American Business Vocabulary

John Flower

with

Ron Martínez

Language Teaching Publications
114a Church Rd, Hove, BN3 2EB, England

© Language Teaching Publications 1995
ISBN 0 906717 69 8
Reprinted 1995, 1997, 2000

John Flower

John is a teacher at Eurocentre Bournemouth where he has worked for many years. He would like to thank Michael Lewis for his encouragement and guidance. He would also like to express his thanks to his colleagues and students for all their help, and to Ruth, Helen, and Andrew.

Ron Martínez

Ron is a native of California and has worked extensively as an ESL instructor in San Francisco, Los Angeles, and Valencia, Spain. He is currently teaching at West Virginia University. Ron is responsible for this American edition.

Acknowledgements
Cover design by Anna Macleod.
Cover photograph courtesy of Zefa.
Illustrations By James Slater.
Printed in England by Commercial Colour Press Plc, London E7.

Building your business vocabulary efficiently

So you plan to build your vocabulary! Learning vocabulary is a very important part of learning English. If you make a grammar mistake, it may be "wrong" but very often people will understand you anyway. But if you don't know the exact word that you need, it is very frustrating for you, and the person you are talking to. Good business English means having a big vocabulary!

There are better and worse ways to build your vocabulary and this book will help you to build your vocabulary quickly and effectively.

You will find it is best to work:

* systematically
* regularly
* personally

Don't just make lists of all the new words you encounter – plan and choose. Think of areas **you** are interested in; look for things **you** can't say in English, then fill those gaps in **your** vocabulary.

Think about the kind of vocabulary you need. What about social English? The language of business letters? Reading in special areas such as public relations or international trade? Building your business vocabulary is a big job – you can help yourself by choosing the things that are most use to you and learning those first.

You can also use things you encounter every day at work as a source of useful language. Look at the letters received in your office, read any company literature which is written in English. Use the English around you to improve your English!

Don't just learn words; you also need to know how to use them. Which words does a word often combine with? This book will help you to learn more words, but also how to use the words you know more effectively. That is an important part of building your vocabulary.

Don't use your dictionary only when you have a problem. It is an important resource. It can help you in lots of different ways. There are tips all through this book to help you use your dictionary effectively.

Don't just make lists of new words; organize them. Again, there are tips to help you to learn and remember more of what you study.

John Flower

Contents

1.   Using a dictionary 6
2.   Word groups – 1 8
3.   In the office – 1 9
4.   Letters – 1 Inquiries 10
5.   Word partnerships – 1 11
6.   Past tense – 1 12
7.   Using the Yellow Pages 13
8.   Confusing words – 1 14
9.   Banking services 15
10. Social English – 1 16
11. Letters – 2 Answering inquiries 18
12. Two-word expressions – 1 19
13. Product information 20
14. Word formation – 1 22
15. Opposites – 1 24
16. Word partnerships – 2 25
17. Mr Baker's trip 26
18. Letters – 3 Orders 28
19. Word groups – 2 29
20. The electronic office 30
21. Make or do? 31
22. Problems, problems 32
23. Letters – 4 Delayed orders 34
24. Special areas – 1 Buying and selling 35
25. Metaphors in Business – 1 36
26. Organization chart 37
27. Giving a presentation 38
28. Word partnerships – 3 40
29. Choose the adverb – 1 41
30. Special areas – 2 Public relations 42
31. Letters – 5 Sales 43
32. Advertising – 1 44
33. Opposites – 2 45
34. Word formation – 2 46
35. Formal English 48

36.	Special areas – 3 Investing	49
37.	Social English – 2	50
38.	Applying for a job	52
39.	Past tense – 2	54
40.	Special areas – 4 Accounting	55
41.	Important adjectives	56
42.	Word partnerships – 4	57
43.	Special areas – 5 Labor relations	58
44.	In the office – 2	59
45.	Noun and preposition	60
46.	Two-word expressions – 2	61
47.	What's the job?	62
48.	Special areas – 6 Insurance	64
49.	Expressions with 'take'	65
50.	Business Jargon	66
51.	Confusing words – 2	67
52.	Word formation – 3	68
53.	Special areas – 7 International trade	70
54.	Color idioms	71
55.	Adjective and preposition	72
56.	Word partnerships – 5	73
57.	Special areas – 8 Personnel	74
58.	Expressions with 'in'	76
59.	Advertising – 2	77
60.	Letters – 6 Exhibition information	78
61.	Word partnerships – 6	79
62.	Social English – 3	80
63.	Special areas – 9 The law	81
64.	Choose the adverb – 2	82
65.	Letters – 7 Booking a hotel room	83
66.	Increasing efficiency	84
67.	Special areas – 10 Management	85
68.	Metaphors in Business – 2	86
	Tests	87
	Answers	92

1 Using a dictionary

If you want to learn business vocabulary, you should have a good English-English dictionary.
Use one with explanations that are easy to understand and which has sentences showing how you use the words.

Practice using a dictionary by answering these questions.

1. Meaning

Which one of these is a kind of office building?

high-tech	**high-end**
high-rise	**high-volume**

Of course a dictionary gives you a definition, but it helps you in other ways too. The next questions show you how.

2. Words which go together

Match a verb on the left with a noun on the right.

Use each word once only.

answer	a check	. . . .
attend	a computer	. . . .
cash	a conference	. . . .
join	the phone	. . . .
program	a team	. . . .

Some words often occur with other words; they form word partnerships. A good dictionary will give examples of the way in which words go together like this.

3. Word formation

Use the correct form of the word COMPETE in each sentence.

His . . . . are worried about his new product line.

She took part in a . . . . to design a new yacht.

We have to be very . . . . to succeed in this business.

This car is more . . . . priced than the other one.

Words often have different grammatical forms. A good dictionary will show you these.

4. The past tense

Complete the sentence by using the past tense of the verb in parentheses.

She . . . . $300 out of the bank. (DRAW)

In the past we . . . . the market in office equipment. (LEAD)

Last year profits . . . . by 20%. (RISE)

The strike soon . . . . to other departments. (SPREAD)

Y ou need to know when a word is irregular; again your dictionary should help you.

5. Abbreviations

What do the following abbreviations mean?

approx.	. . . .
Co.	. . . .
ATM	. . . .
FOB	. . . .
PO Box	. . . .
NAFTA	. . . .

A bbreviations are used quite often in business so it is important to look up and note down any new ones you encounter. You should also know how to say each abbreviation. A good dictionary should tell you this.

6. Pronunciation

Which of these words has a different vowel sound?

a.	gone	loan	own	phone
b.	fair	gear	share	wear
c.	could	food	goods	should
d.	freight	height	state	weight

Y ou don't really know a word until you know how to say it properly. This is why a good dictionary shows you the pronunciation of each word.

2 Word groups – 1

It is useful to make a list of the words you use when you talk about a subject. When you learn a new word, you can add it to your list.
This book will give you some ideas but why not think of some areas of business you are interested in and see how many words you can think of?

Put each of the words below into the correct list.

Use each word once only.

Can you think of any more words to add to each list?

agenda	classified ad.	minutes	reservation
CEO	commercial (n)	overtime	room service
apply for	exchange rate	owe	stapler
campaign	fax	slogan	computer
chairperson	filing cabinet	profit	training
check in	interview	refund	weekend rate

1. Advertising

. . . .

. . . .

. . . .

. . . .

2. Hotel

. . . .

. . . .

. . . .

. . . .

3. Job

. . . .

. . . .

. . . .

. . . .

4. Meeting

. . . .

. . . .

. . . .

. . . .

5. Money

. . . .

. . . .

. . . .

. . . .

6. The office

. . . .

. . . .

. . . .

. . . .

3 In the office – 1

Look at the picture of an office. From the list below find the word for each numbered item. Use each word once only.

calendar	filing cabinet	pen	eraser
check book	keyboard	pencil	umbrella
appointment book	map	phone	vase
files	passport	printer	monitor

1. . . . .   2. . . . .   3. . . . .   4. . . . .

5. . . . .   6. . . . .   7. . . . .   8. . . . .

9. . . . .   10. . . . .   11. . . . .   12. . . . .

13. . . . .   14. . . . .   15. . . . .   16. . . . .

4 Letters – 1 Inquiries

If you receive any business letters in English, use them to learn more vocabulary. Note down any useful words and phrases and then try to write similar letters of your own. In the same way, write your own letters based on those that you find in this book.

Below you will see parts of three letters of inquiry. Put the correct word or phrase in each blank. Choose from the following list. Use each item once only.

advertisement	discount	latest catalog	price list
advise	sincerely	model	price range
current issue	forward	particularly	regards
Dear	information	payment	still available

A.

1. . . . . Sir or Madam

I saw your **2.** . . . . in the **3.** . . . . of 'Office Weekly' and am interested in your selection of office stationery.

Could you please send me your **4.** . . . . and **5.** . . . . I look **6.** . . . . to hearing from you.

7. . . . .

B.

With **8.** . . . . to your advertisement in today's 'Washington Post', could you please send me **9.** . . . . about your office furniture. I am **10.** . . . . interested in your adjustable secretary's chairs.

C.

Some time ago we purchased from you some JF72 solar-powered pocket calculators.

As this **11.** . . . . was so popular with our customers, we would like to know if it is **12.** . . . . If so, would you kindly **13.** . . . . us of your terms of **14.** . . . . and any quantity **15.** . . . . available. Could you also include details on any new models in the same **16.** . . . .

5 Word partnerships – 1

Some pairs of words often occur together. If you encounter one, you can expect the other. This makes it easier to understand written and spoken English.

Match each verb on the left with a noun on the right to form common partnerships. Use each word once only. Write your answers in the boxes.

Set 1

1. answer	**a.** a profit
2. appoint	**b.** a letter
3. call	**c.** a meeting
4. make	**d.** a new manager
5. raise	**e.** the phone
6. solve	**f.** a problem
7. type	**g.** capital
8. entertain	**h.** a client

1	
2	
3	
4	
5	
6	
7	
8	

Set 2

Now do the same with these words.

1. fill	**a.** an applicant
2. interview	**b.** a business
3. offer	**c.** a contract
4. owe	**d.** a discount
5. rent	**e.** some money
6. run	**f.** office space
7. send	**g.** a fax
8. sign	**h.** an order

1	
2	
3	
4	
5	
6	
7	
8	

Now complete each sentence using a suitable expression from above.

1. They might . . . . if you pay within ten days.

2. Despite problems in the past, we can . . . . this year.

3. They're trying to . . . . for their new business.

4. The CEO will . . . . on Tuesday to discuss the new proposal.

6 Past tense – 1

Most verbs in English form their past by adding 'd' or 'ed' but there are also about 200 irregular verbs in English. About 100 of these are common so you should always check the past tense of any verb you learn.

Complete each of the sentences by using the past form of one of the verbs on the left and combining it with one of the words on the right. Use each verb once only. Some words on the right are used more than once.

break	find	keep	shut		back	off	through
build	get	fall	take		down	on	up
cut	go	read	think		from	out	over
come	hear	sell	drive				

1. By accident the switchboard operator . . . . her . . . . in the middle of our conversation.

2. After testing everything they finally . . . . what was wrong with the machine.

3. They . . . . costs . . . . by using less expensive materials.

4. DSI . . . . with a new multi-media computer to compete in that competitive market.

5. He . . . . the figures . . . . to her so that she could be sure that he had the quantities exactly right.

6. Because of a conflict of interest, the deal . . . .

7. They . . . . the offer . . . . for a week before making a decision.

8. After calling three times I finally . . . . to home office.

9. She . . . . her business . . . . from one small shop to a chain of department stores.

10. The packing equipment . . . . and production was halted for an hour.

11. The new selection was so popular that the store . . . . in 2 days.

12. Last year they . . . . the factory for three weeks and everybody had to take their vacation at the same time.

13. She . . . . working even though the others had stopped.

14. High interest rates . . . . real estate prices during the first quarter of last year.

15. My plane . . . . four hours late because of fog.

16. I finally . . . . our agent in Turkey. He phoned last week.

7 Using the yellow pages

In the yellow pages of a telephone directory, services and suppliers are listed under appropriate headings.
In this exercise you have to decide which heading from the following list you would look under for what you need. Use each heading once only.
Write your answers in the boxes.

1. ACCOUNTANTS
2. ADVERTISING AGENCIES
3. AIR CHARTER & RENTAL
4. COLLECTION AGENCIES
5. HOTELS
6. INTERIOR DESIGNERS

7. LAWYERS
8. OFFICE FURNITURE
9. RESTAURANTS
10. SECURITY SERVICES
11. STATIONERY SUPPLIERS
12. TRAVEL AGENTS

PROBLEM

a. You want to take a client out to dinner.	1
b. A visiting businessman wants somewhere to stay.	2
c. You're worried about your tax liabilities.	3
d. You're going to launch a new product onto the market.	4
e. You want to book a flight.	5
f. You're worried about industrial espionage.	6
g. You've run out of typing paper.	7
h. A secretary needs a new chair.	8
i. Several customers have still not settled their accounts.	9
j. You want to rent a helicopter.	10
k. The reception area looks dull.	11
l. You are being sued for negligence.	12

Now complete each of the following sentences with a suitable phrase from the sentences you have just seen.

1. This new process is top secret and they're worried about . . . .

2. She's calling the travel agency to . . . .

3. The clients who still hadn't . . . . were sent a final reminder.

4. They're holding a reception to . . . . onto the market.

5. Could you book a table at La Dolce Vita? I want to take Mr East . . . .

8 Confusing words – 1

If you use a word in the wrong way, learn from your mistake. Find out what the correct word or expression should be and then use both the correct and incorrect words in sentences so that you can understand and remember the differences.

Choose the correct word for each sentence.

1. She works for an **advertisement/advertising** agency.

2. How will the increase in interest rates **affect/effect** your sales?

3. My bank manager has agreed to **borrow/lend** me another $2,000.

4. We've had to **cancel/postpone** the meeting until next Monday.

5. These machines are **controlled/inspected** at least once a day.

6. My plane was **delayed/postponed** by an hour due to computer failure.

7. Before coming here, I studied **economics/economy** in college.

8. I'm **interested/interesting** in their new camera.

9. She applied for a **job/work** as a director of human resources.

10. Environmentalists watch carefully what businesses do with industrial **waste/waist**.

11. The cost of **life/living** has gone up again.

12. Please send precise **measurements/measures** when ordering.

13. We expect prices to **raise/rise** by at least five per cent.

14. We only exchange goods if you produce a **receipt/recipe**.

15. I must **remember/remind** the boss about that meeting this afternoon.

16. Can you **say/tell** the difference between these two products?

17. The company is extremely **sensible/sensitive** to any criticism.

18. There's some more paper in the **stationary/stationery** cabinet.

9 Banking services

One way of building your vocabulary is to ask yourself how many words you can write down about a certain subject. After you have made your list, and checked the spelling and pronunciation, you can add any new words you encounter. Before you do this exercise, see how many words you can write down on the subject of banking. After you have done the exercise, add any new words to your list.

Fill each blank in the text with the correct word or phrase. Choose from the following list. Use each item once only.

commission	debited	in full	interest
issued	outstanding	statement	withdraw
credit rating	ATM	loan	default
collateral	bounce	overdraft	financial institutions

Banks offer many services to businesses and their customers. Here are some of the most common:

Many people now have a card which enables them to **1.** . . . . money from an **2.** . . . . You feed your card into the machine and key in your PIN (personal identification number) and the amount of money you want. If you have enough in your account, the amount requested will be **3.** . . . . to you up to a daily limit. Your account is automatically **4.** . . . . for the amount you have drawn out.

Provided you have a sound **5.** . . . ., you can get a credit card from a bank and other **6.** . . . . To obtain goods or services, you present your card and sign a special voucher. When it receives the voucher, the credit card company pays the merchant minus a **7.** . . . . and then sends you a monthly **8.** . . . . Depending on the type of card you have, you will either have to pay **9.** . . . . or be able to pay part of what is owed and pay **10.** . . . . on the balance left **11.** . . . .

If you need additional money for investments or other major purchases, you can take out a **12.** . . . . The bank may need you to offer them something as **13.** . . . . in case you **14.** . . . . on your loan. Most good banks offer checking accounts with **15.** . . . . protection so that a check won't **16.** . . . . in case no funds are available in your account.

10 Social English – 1

In business there are times when you need to speak English socially, for example when you go out for a meal with an English-speaking client or colleague. It is important, therefore, to know some of the expressions used in these more informal situations. As you do this exercise, try to imagine situations in which these exchanges could occur.

Complete each of these conversations with an appropriate response from the list below. Use each response once only.

Responses

a. Nice to meet you. I'm Jane Ford.
b. Already?
c. Thanks. You too.
d. Congratulations!
e. No problem. It's my pleasure.
f. No thanks. I just had one.
g. Yes, very much, thanks.
h. Not much better, I'm afraid.
i. Only a few days.
j. It sure is.
k. That would be great, thanks.
l. Can I give you a hand?

1. . . . .

2. . . . .

3. . . . .

4. . . . .

5. . . . .

6. . . . .

7. . . . .

8. . . . .

9. . . . .

10. . . . .

11. . . . .

12. . . . .

11 Letters – 2
Answering inquiries

Below you will see parts of three letters answering an inquiry. Put the correct word or phrase in each blank. Choose from the following list. Use each item once only.

additional features	enclosed leaflet	further details	pleasure
competitive price	inquiring	hesitate	selection
date	inquiry	In addition	Sincerely
doing business	full details	in production	supply

A.

Dear Ms Prentice

Thank you for your **1.**........ of May 3rd about our office stationery.

It is our **2.**........ to enclose our latest catalog and price list. We hope you will find it of interest.

If you require any **3.**........, please do not **4.**........ to contact us.

5......... .

B.

Thank you for your letter of January 4th, asking about office furniture.

The enclosed catalog contains **6.**........ of our selection. In most cases we are able to **7.**........ you with the goods you require within fourteen days.

We look forward to hearing from you.

C.

Thank you for your letter of June 1st, **8.**........ about the JF72 pocket calculator.

This model is no longer **9.**........ as it has been superseded by the JF73 solar-powered pocket calculator. As you will see from the **10.**........, the new model has several **11.**........ at an extremely **12.**........ .

We have also enclosed our latest catalog giving details of the wide **13.**........ of electronic goods we supply.

We provide a discount of 30% on purchases of not less than 50 of the same model, and 35% on quantities of not less than 100. **14.**........, we give a discount of 3% for payment within fourteen days from **15.**........ of invoice.

We look forward to **16.**........ with you in the near future.

12 Two-word expressions – 1

Sometimes in English two words are used together to make a common expression, for example:

credit card   **departure lounge**

Sometimes you'll find these expressions listed separately in a dictionary and sometimes they are included in the definitions of one, or both, of the words. You need to learn the expressions as complete phrases.

Join one word on the left with one from the right to make a two-word partnership. Use each word once only. Write your answers in the boxes.

1. trade	**a.** building		1	
2. cash	**b.** board		2	
3. government	**c.** cabinet		3	
4. worker	**d.** productivity		4	
5. exchange	**e.** exchange		5	
6. filing	**f.** flow		6	
7. income	**g.** margin		7	
8. insurance	**h.** show		8	
9. customer	**i.** policy		9	
10. bulletin	**j.** processor		10	
11. office	**k.** rate		11	
12. profit	**l.** satisfaction		12	
13. stock	**m.** worker		13	
14. labor	**n.** tax		14	
15. word	**o.** union		15	

Now complete each sentence with one of the expressions.

1. She bought a . . . . to replace her old typewriter.

2. They built a big . . . . in the middle of town.

3. Change your money when the . . . . is more favorable.

4. . . . . is very important for the success of our business.

13 Product information

If you can get catalogs in English, or magazines or newspapers containing advertisements in English, look at the descriptions of the products. You can find a lot of useful vocabulary this way.

In addition, many products have information written in English which will also help you to build your vocabulary. Remember, there are many opportunities to see real English. All of them can help you to learn.

In this exercise you will see some information about a product. You must decide which product is being referred to. Choose the product from the following list. Each product is referred to once only.

answering machine	**computer**	**laser printer**	**photocopier**
briefcase	**cordless phone**	**office chair**	**pocket calculator**
burglar alarm	**daily planner**	**pager**	**signmaking kit**
clock	**fax machine**	**pen**	**table lamp**

Desktop publishing at an affordable price. High resolution. Compatible with a wide range of systems.

With built-in pre-recorded message or facility to record your own. Speaker volume control.

1. . . . .

2. . . . .

The infa-red sensors detect any intruders. A message is immediately sent to the control.

Make calls anywhere inside or within 100 feet outside. Paging feature.

3. . . . .

4. . . . .

60 gray shades for better transmission of photographs. One touch dialling.

High resolution color monitor. Comes complete with word-processing and other business software.

5. . . . .

6. . . . .

Stylish cover. Page a day. Contains conversion tables and other useful information.

Swivel base. With or without arms. Fully adjustable. Variety of fabrics. Extra deep cushioning.

7. . . . .

8. . . . .

Receives messages up to 45 miles. 4 lines text. Beep or vibrate mode.

The effective answer to high volume duplication. Adjustable speeds. Quality reproduction.

9. . . . .

10. . . . .

Durable self-adhesive letters, numbers and symbols in a variety of sizes. Can be used indoors and out.

White face with black numerals. Battery included.

11. . . . .

12. . . . .

Document folio in lid. Pockets for calculator, pens etc. Combination locks.

Solar powered. 8-digit LCD display.

13. . . . .

14. . . . .

Stainless steel cap and barrel. Supplied with blue refill.

Fully adjustable. Reach 30 in. Max 60 watt bulb.

15. . . . .

16. . . . .

Now look through the descriptions and note down any words or phrases that will be useful for you.

14 Word formation – 1

When you look up a word in a dictionary, see if you can form other words from it. Sometimes these words will be included in the definition of the word and sometimes they will appear separately. Look before and after each dictionary entry to see what words you can find formed from the same basic word.

Complete each sentence with the correct form of the word in capital letters. In some cases you will have to make a negative form by using the prefix **in-** or **un-**.

1. ACCEPT

   I'm sorry, but this arrangement is totally . . . . to us.

   I've just received their letter of . . . . so we can go ahead.

2. ACT

   The unions have threatened to take industrial . . . .

   It's been a very . . . . day on Wall Street.

   The R&D department seems full of . . . . at the moment.

3. ADD

   We'll be bringing out several . . . . to our product line.

   There's an . . . . bonus if I exceed my sales target by more than 10%.

4. ANALYZE

   We'll need a detailed cost . . . . before giving final approval.

   Most . . . . think we're in for a difficult time.

5. APPLY

   Unfortunately we can't interview every . . . .

   I sent in my letter of . . . . and they phoned me the next day.

   The regulations are not . . . . when there are fewer than 10 employees.

6. ASSIST

   We'll need some financial . . . . to enable us to buy more stock.

   He was in a meeting so I spoke to the . . . . manager.

7. ATTRACT

   One of the . . . . of the offer is the free training course.

   They were offering a very . . . . salary so of course I was interested.

8. COMMERCE

There are so many . . . . vehicles on the road these days!

I'm afraid the operation is not . . . . viable.

The resort has become so . . . . that we're going somewhere else.

In addition to newspaper advertising, we plan a series of TV . . . .

9. CONNECT

My . . . . flight didn't leave until 10 o'clock.

We sent them a letter in . . . . with their offer of an agency.

She has some useful . . . . in the hotel trade.

10. CONTRACT

The . . . . has told me the office will be ready by next month.

We are . . . . obliged to provide adequate security for the shipment.

11. DIRECT

I enclose a map and . . . . to help you to find our office.

The board of . . . . will make the final decision about the operation.

I found the company by looking in the local telephone . . . .

I always deal . . . . with the manufacturer.

There's been another . . . . from home office about photocopying.

12. DECIDE

He'll never make a good manager. He's so . . . .

A . . . . on the new factory is expected soon.

13. COMPETE

I worry about industrial espionage from our . . . .

There is some fierce . . . . in this business.

With such a narrow profit margin, it's hard to keep our prices . . . .

14. DISTRIBUTE

He's the sole . . . . in this area, so we're forced to buy from him.

The increase in gas prices will drive up our . . . . costs.

15. ECONOMY

We must . . . . on electricity, so turn off those lights.

All those wonderful . . . . haven't found a solution to our problems.

15 Opposites – 1

When you see an adjective in a sentence, ask yourself if it's possible to replace it by its opposite. You will notice that some adjectives have several opposites depending on the context.

The opposite of *short*, for example, could be *long* or *tall*. Can you think of any more examples like this? A good dictionary will help you. It's another word partnership problem!

Complete each sentence with the opposite of the word in parentheses. Choose from the following list. Use each word once only.

approximate	**full-time**	**marked**	**private**
basic	**internal**	**negative**	**short**
complex	**light**	**partial**	
mandatory	**low**	**permanent**	

1. The new complaints procedure has been a . . . . success. (COMPLETE)

2. Do you have the . . . . sales figures? (EXACT)

3. The position went to an . . . . candidate. (EXTERNAL)

4. I didn't expect my salary to be this . . . . ! (HIGH)

5. There's a lot of . . . . industry in the area. (HEAVY)

6. We're expecting big savings in the . . . . term. (LONG)

7. Wearing a tie was . . . . in his office. (OPTIONAL)

8. She has a . . . . job as an Account Executive. (PART-TIME)

9. There was a very . . . . reaction to my suggestion. (POSITIVE)

10. Wages have risen more slowly in the . . . . sector. (PUBLIC)

11. The company has a . . . . management structure. (SIMPLE)

12. There was a . . . . improvement in efficiency. (SLIGHT)

13. We could see he was using very . . . . equipment. (SOPHISTICATED)

14. He's got himself a . . . . job as a mechanic. (TEMPORARY)

16 Word partnerships – 2

Match each adjective on the left with a noun on the right to form common partnerships. Use each word once only. Write your answers in the boxes.

Set 1

1. annual	a. conference		1	
2. early	b. marketing		2	
3. direct	c. dismissal		3	
4. limited	d. enterprise		4	
5. natural	e. liability		5	
6. savvy	f. investor		6	
7. private	g. resources		7	
8. unfair	h. retirement		8	

Set 2

Now do the same with these words.

1. effective	a. communication		1	
2. financial	b. difficulties		2	
3. high	c. investment		3	
4. introductory	d. offer		4	
5. skilled	e. priority		5	
6. sound	f. property		6	
7. vacant	g. selection		7	
8. wide	h. workers		8	

Now complete each sentence using an appropriate expression from above.

1. As a special . . . . , they're selling two for the price of one.

2. I'm going to the . . . . of our labor union.

3. He was only 50 but he decided to take . . . .

4. There is a shortage of . . . . for this kind of work.

25

17 Mr Baker's trip

Below you will see pictures of different stages in Mr Baker's trip. You must decide which of the sentences below goes with which picture. Use each sentence once only.

a.   Thanks a lot for all your help.

b.   I have an appointment with Miss Jarvis.

c.   I'd like to reserve a room under the name of Baker.

d.   Keep the change.

e.   This is the last call for flight QF2, now boarding at Gate 24.

f.   How was your trip?

g.   Do you have anything to declare, sir?

h.   A round trip to Chicago, please.

i.   Medium, please.

j.   The Hotel Major, please.

k.   My name's Baker. My secretary has booked a room for me.

l.   Nice to meet you.

m.   Here's to our continued co-operation.

n.   I'm afraid there's been a mistake. I'm sure my secretary booked a room for me.

1. . . . .

2. . . . .

3. . . . .

4. . . . .

5. . . . .

6. . . . .

7. . . . .

8. . . . .

9. . . . .

10. . . . .

11. . . . .

12. . . . .

13. . . . .

14. . . . .

18 Letters – 3 Orders

Below you will see parts of four letters concerned with orders. Put the correct word or phrase in each blank. Choose from the following list. Use each item once only.

accept delivery	inconvenience	selection	quotation
acknowledge	line	regret	inventory
current issue	note	reserve the right	supply
following	shipping	resume	terms

A.

With reference to your advertisement in the **1.**........of 'Office Monthly', I would like to order 2 Easifix Year Planners.

I enclose a check for $15 to include **2.**........and handling.

B.

Thank you for your **3.**........of July 5th for your "Finesse" **4.**........of dining room furniture. We find your **5.**........satisfactory and would like to order the **6.**........ .

        10 "Finesse" dining tables at $280 per item
        40 "Finesse" dining chairs at $60 per item

We **7.**........that you can supply these items within 30 days and we **8.**........not to **9.**........after this time.

We would be grateful if you would **10.**........receipt of this order.

C.

We thank you for your order of May 11th for 2 Easifix Year Planners.

This **11.**........ has proved so popular that we **12.**........ to inform you that it is temporarily out of stock.

We hope to be able to **13.**........ supplies within the next ten days.

We apologize for any **14.**........ this may cause.

D.

Thank you for your order of July 12th for 10 "Finesse" dining tables and 40 "Finesse" dining chairs.

As we are in a position to **15.**........you with the above items from **16.**........, we have arranged for them to be delivered to you early next week.

19 Word groups – 2

Remember that grouping together words connected with the same topic can help you to learn them. As you encounter new vocabulary, see if you can think of other words that could be used in the same context.

Put each of the words below into the correct list.
Some words could go into more than one list but use each word once only and put it into the category with which it is most commonly associated.
Can you think of any more words to add to each list?

adjuster	dumping	picket	speculate
portfolio	embargo	policyholder	stock exchange
claim	export	premium	strike
lay-offs	judge	E-mail	sue
compatible	legal	shares	tariff
data	mediate	software	trial

1. Computers

. . . .

. . . .

. . . .

. . . .

2. Labor relations

. . . .

. . . .

. . . .

. . . .

3. Insurance

. . . .

. . . .

. . . .

. . . .

4. International trade

. . . .

. . . .

. . . .

. . . .

5. Investing

. . . .

. . . .

. . . .

. . . .

6. The law

. . . .

. . . .

. . . .

. . . .

20 The electronic office

In this passage about the use of computers in business you must fill each blank with one word. Choose each word from the following list. You must use each word once only.

accurate	records	on-line	peripherals
publishing	memory	transactions	supplies
graphics	retrieve	display	printer
networking	back-up	drive	components

USING COMPUTERS

Computers are being used more and more in business because they are fast, efficient and **1.** . . . .

Here are some ways in which computers are used:

Insurance companies use them to store and **2.** . . . . details of clients' policies.

Production departments in companies use them to ensure they have adequate **3.** . . . . of raw materials and **4.** . . . .

Banks use them for processing details of accounts and **5.** . . . .

Personnel departments use them to keep **6.** . . . . of a company's employees.

For the most part, the computers, software, and **7.** . . . . that are needed depend on individual needs. For instance, if you're an architect you may want a system with good **8.** . . . . capability. If a lot of records are to be kept, then you'll want ample **9.** . . . . , perhaps even a CD-ROM **10.** . . . . for permanent storage of massive amounts of data. Regular disks can then be used for **11.** . . . . copies. For desktop **12.** . . . . , you may want a monitor with a full-page **13.** . . . . and a high-quality laser **14.** . . . . If quality printing is not so important, then a cheaper ink-jet or even cheaper dot-matrix printer may be more suitable.

If you're in a business where you need to do a lot of **15.** . . . . , then maybe you should consider a modem, so you can communicate with other computers **16.** . . . .

21 Make or do?

Complete each sentence with the correct form of 'make' or 'do'.

1. There's a rumor going around that Empire Inc. is going to . . . . a bid for Squash International.

2. Please . . . . your best to get these typed before 5 o'clock.

3. Who should I . . . . the check out to?

4. These new sales figures show we've already . . . . up for last quarter's losses.

5. I'm afraid you'll have to . . . . without the other photocopier until we can get the part we need from the suppliers.

6. We've been . . . . business with them for over thirty years now.

7. Considerable progress has been . . . . and we hope to give some concrete proposals to our members tomorrow afternoon.

8. It's important to . . . . a good first impression for potential clients.

9. They've been . . . . really good business since they decided to advertise on local television.

10. We have . . . . a considerable profit on the sale of that land.

11. I've got all these invoices to . . . . before I can go home.

12. The business was so run down when she took it over that nobody expected her to . . . . such a success of it.

13. Something as simple as changing the size of the lettering on the packet can . . . . all the difference to your sales.

14. Increasing production will . . . . even more demands on machinery which is already breaking down at an alarming rate.

15. They could . . . . with some computer paper in the payroll office.

16. We've . . . . away with the old system of punching in.

17. A customer has . . . . a complaint about one of our salespeople.

18. In fact, Gravers has . . . . us a favor by launching their product first. We can learn from their mistakes.

When you have checked your answers, underline each expression with 'do' or 'make' to help you to remember them.

22 Problems, problems

My Secretary keeps complaining
of a bad back.
– If I were you, I'd get
her a better chair.

Match each sentence below with the best response on the next page.
Use each response once only.

1. . . . .

2. . . . .

3. . . . .

4. . . . .

5. . . . .

6. . . . .

7. . . . .

8. . . . .

9. . . . .

10. . . . .

11. . . . .

12. . . . .

a. Let's see what R & D can come up with.
b. Should I get you some more from the stationery store?
c. Why don't you look for a job abroad?
d. Have you tried getting one from an employment agency?
e. They say there's still growth left in the leisure industry.
f. How about Tuesday morning?

g. I'd give them another call if I were you.
h. Do you think arbitration would help?
i. Maybe they'll accept partial payment.
j. In that case, you'd better send it registered.
k. Do you want me to look through them for you?
l. Why not fax them, then?

23 Letters – 4 Delayed orders

Below you will see parts of three letters concerned with a delay in fulfilling an order. Put the correct word or phrase in each blank. Choose from the following list. Use each item once only.

apologize for	deter	misplaced	refund
dealing	further delay	obliged	regret the delay
deducted	issue	passed	response
processing	matter	guaranteed delivery	set

A.

On October 8th I sent you an order for a **1.** . . . . of five computer programs which you had advertised in the October **2.** . . . . of 'Computer World'.

Although your advertisement **3.** . . . . within 28 days, 6 weeks have now **4.** . . . . and I have still not received the programs. You must have received my order as the $70 I paid by check has been **5.** . . . . from my bank account.

Would you please look into this **6.** . . . . for me and send my order without **7.** . . . .

B.

Two weeks ago I sent you a letter inquiring about my order of October 8th for five computer programs which had not arrived.

I have received no **8.** . . . . to my letter and the programs have still not been delivered. I must ask you, therefore, either to send my order immediately or to **9.** . . . . my payment of $70.

I hope I will not be **10.** . . . . to take this matter any further.

C.

Thank you for your letter of November 23rd. We **11.** . . . . in **12.** . . . . your order for the five computer programs.

Unfortunately, we had problems with our new computerized system for **13.** . . . . with orders and, as a result, your order was **14.** . . . .

We have enclosed the five programs you ordered together with an extra disk which we hope will go some way to making up for the delay.

Once again we **15.** . . . . the inconvenience. We hope that it will not **16.** . . . . you from doing business with us in the future.

24 Special areas – 1
Buying and selling

Choose the best alternative to complete the sentence.

1. As soon as an item of stock falls below its minimum . . . ., the computer automatically re-orders.
   a. standard **b.** level **c.** grade **d.** position

2. Often a discount is offered as an . . . . to get a customer to pay promptly.
   a. investment **b.** incentive **c.** interim **d.** inventory

3. Remember that was only an . . . . The final cost could be higher.
   a. inquiry **b.** estimate **c.** encouragement **d.** engagement

4. Check the . . . . invoice and see that you've got everything.
   a. deliver **b.** delivered **c.** delivery **d.** delivering

5. When ordering, please quote the . . . .
   a. numbered catalog **b.** catalog **c.** figure **d.** catalog number

6. Let's do another . . . . to announce our new product.
   a. mailing **b.** mailer **c.** package **d.** mail

7. Every month account customers are sent a . . . .
   a. final demand **b.** statement **c.** request **d.** stocktaking

8. In the UK, VAT (value added tax) is a tax on goods and . . . .
   a. services **b.** servants **c.** stockings **d.** stockists

9. If they don't . . . . their account we'll take them to court.
   a. set up **b.** pay up **c.** settle **d.** pay for

10. By mistake we have undercharged her so we'll have to send her a . . . . note for the amount.
    a. debt **b.** credit **c.** debit **d.** credit-worthy

11. If you take the sweater back to the store they'll want to see the . . . . to show you bought it there.
    a. receipt **b.** reception **c.** permit **d.** quotation

12. It's a . . . . market at the moment so you should be able to pick some up at a reasonable price.
    a. open **b.** free **c.** buyer's **d.** seller's

13. The market has reached . . . . point so we need to concentrate on finding new products.
    a. full **b.** saturation **c.** filling **d.** boiling

14. We hope that business will . . . . when the tourist season starts.
    a. set off **b.** get up **c.** pick up **d.** pick off

15. You'll probably find furniture polish among the . . . . goods.
    a. house **b.** housing **c.** household **d.** housewife

16. They've pulled down the old market and built a shopping . . . .
    a. premises **b.** mall **c.** franchise **d.** retailer

25 Metaphors in Business – 1

A metaphor is when you say one thing is something else. For example a metaphor in business English is:

Time is money!

In English metaphors like this are very common. If you pay close attention, you may notice that language that is usually associated with money can often be used when talking about time.

Choose from these verbs to complete the sentences below. Use each verb once only.

borrow	**invest**	**save**
buy	**budget**	**spare**
find	**lose**	**spend**
give	**make**	**waste**

1. I need for the Board of Directors to . . . . me some more time to finish the project.

2. Being in management doesn't allow one to . . . . time with fellow employees.

3. If you want to be efficient you need to . . . . your time carefully.

4. By traveling by train we were able to . . . . a lot of time.

5. Judging by the potential of this growing technology, I feel it would be wise to . . . . some time in research.

6. Don't . . . . your time with that calculator. It's faster if you do it on the computer.

7. By promising better results if the committee extended her project deadline, Natalie was able to . . . . some more time.

8. Though he knew he had to work a full shift that day, he needed to . . . . some time from his boss to visit his wife in the hospital.

9. I've got a busy schedule on Monday, but I'll . . . . some time for your appointment in the morning.

10. With so much work to do I can't seem to . . . . any time to have fun.

11. We would've been finished today, but unfortunately, we . . . . a lot of time when the computers broke down.

12. Seeing that we only have one week left before the exhibition, there's absolutely no time to . . . .

Can you use each of the above verbs in sentences with 'money'?

Did you remember to underline word partnerships like 'busy schedule'?

26 Organization chart

Think about the ways in which companies are organized into departments with different responsibilities. Do you know the names in English of the people in charge and how to talk about their responsibilities? If not, try to find out and then make your own chart similar to the one below.

Below you will see a chart showing the way in which a company could be organized. In some cases, a word is missing from the chart. Find the correct word from the following list. Use each word once only. Write your answers at the bottom of the page.

Corporate　　**Strategic**　　**Officer**　　　**Division**
Directors　　**Resources**　　**Advertising**　　**President**
Finance　　　**Research**　　**Data**　　　　**Development**

```
                         ┌─────────────┐
                         │  Board of   │
                         │ 1. .......  │
                         └──────┬──────┘
                         ┌──────┴──────┐
                         │Chief Executive│
                         │ 2. .......  │
                         └──────┬──────┘
                         ┌──────┴──────┐
                         │  3. ....... │
                         └──────┬──────┘
```

Vice-President 4.	Vice-President 5. .... Relations	Vice-President Administration	Vice-President Corporate 9.	Vice-President International 12. ....
Treasurer	6.	Human 7.	8. .... Processing	10. .... Planning	Economic 11. ....

The missing words are:

1. . . . .　　2. . . . .　　3. . . . .　　4. . . . .

5. . . . .　　6. . . . .　　7. . . . .　　8. . . . .

9. . . . .　　10. . . . .　　11. . . . .　　12. . . . .

When speaking, you say, "I'm Vice-President in-charge-of Finance."

27 Giving a presentation

A.

Look at the picture. Put the correct number by each of these items.

bar graph	**felt pen**	**handout** . . . .
pointer	**curtain**	**flip chart** . . . .
pie chart	**screen**	**slide projector** . . . .
notes	**podium**	**overhead projector** . . . .
line graph	**microphone**	

B.

Below you will see extracts from a presentation. You must complete each blank with a word or phrase from the list below. Use each item from the list once only.

purpose	First of all,	up to date	on such short notice
priorities	Let me start	to sum up	On the contrary,
Finally,	As you know,	as a whole	On the other hand,
Next,	In other words,	As far as	draw your attention

1. . . . . by welcoming you all, especially since this meeting has had to be called 2. . . . .

3. . . . . , our latest project has been the target of intense speculation in the media during the last few days, and the 4. . . . . of this presentation is to bring you 5. . . . . on what has been happening.

6. . . . . , I'd like to refresh your memories as to the background of the project. 7. . . . . , I'll give you a broad outline of what we've achieved so far.
8. . . . . , I'll try to give an indication of what our 9. . . . . will be over the next few months.

If I can 10. . . . . to the month of July, you will notice that there was an unexpected fall in overseas sales.

11. . . . . domestic sales are concerned, you can see that growth has been sustained.

If we look at the figures for Latin America 12. . . . . , and Mexico in particular, we can see some quite encouraging trends.

We don't fear competition. 13. . . . . , we welcome it.

We could open a branch there. 14. . . . . , we may be better advised to look for a good agent to represent us.

This is a time when we must consider our options carefully. 15. . . . . , we should not rush into making any decisions.

So, 16. . . . . then, don't believe everything the media tells you. We've had a few problems but the future looks bright.

28 Word partnerships – 3

Match each verb on the left with a noun on the right to form common partnerships. Use each word once only. Write your answers in the boxes.

Set 1

1.	address	**a.**	a client	**1**	
2.	launch	**b.**	a product	**2**	
3.	consider	**c.**	an employee	**3**	
4.	fire	**d.**	an invoice	**4**	
5.	keep	**e.**	a meeting	**5**	
6.	pay	**f.**	an order	**6**	
7.	place	**g.**	a proposal	**7**	
8.	phone	**h.**	a record	**8**	

Set 2

Now do the same with these words.

1.	build	**a.**	an agreement	**1**	
2.	cash	**b.**	a check	**2**	
3.	process	**c.**	costs	**3**	
4.	express	**d.**	disputes	**4**	
5.	postpone	**e.**	a factory	**5**	
6.	reach	**f.**	an order	**6**	
7.	reduce	**g.**	a meeting	**7**	
8.	settle	**h.**	thanks	**8**	

Now complete each sentence by using a suitable expression from above.

1. They hope to . . . . by employing fewer staff.

2. Companies must do a lot of research before they . . . . onto the market.

3. It's not always easy to . . . . between management and staff.

4. They're going to . . . . on some vacant land nearby.

29 Choose the adverb – 1

As you study English, notice how some adverbs form common partnerships with other words, for example:

Each product is **thoroughly tested.**   This process is **widely used.**

If you want to use English in a natural way, you should note down and learn expressions like this.

From the following list choose a suitable adverb to complete each sentence. Use each adverb once only.

absolutely	**correctly**	**fully**	**tactfully**
environmentally	**eventually**	**satisfactorily**	**temporarily**
considerably	**favorably**	**specially**	**virtually**
conveniently	**financially**	**strictly**	**widely**

1. Our new downtown office is . . . . located in the city's financial district.

2. I hope the negotiations will be concluded . . . .

3. This credit card is . . . . accepted so I take it everywhere.

4. Make sure you're . . . . insured when you go abroad.

5. The accountant had to check that the company was . . . . sound.

6. You have been . . . . selected to try out our latest product.

7. I'm sure the government's policy will . . . . cause a recession.

8. Get this software . . . . free when you buy one of our computers.

9. Entry to this part of the factory is . . . . limited.

10. Production methods vary . . . . from firm to firm.

11. Make sure the envelope is . . . . addressed.

12. The switchboard is . . . . out of order but it'll be soon fixed.

13. The tableware they produce is . . . . unbreakable.

14. She learned how to deal . . . . with people who complained.

15. Our sales figures compare . . . . with those of our competitors.

16. Consumers nowadays look for products that are . . . . friendly.

30 Special areas – 2 Public relations

Choose the best alternative to complete the sentence.

1. The task of the public relations department is to project the right . . . .
   of a company.
   a. painting   **b.** image   **c.** picture   **d.** drawing

2. When the product was launched they issued a press . . . . to all the
   news agencies.
   a. escape   **b.** issue   **c.** release   **d.** promotion

3. According to the code of practice, a public relations officer should not
   knowingly . . . . false information.
   a. disseminate   **b.** dissociate   **c.** dispose   **d.** dissolve

4. Some companies entertain journalists more . . . . than others.
   a. lasciviously   **b.** largely   **c.** leniently   **d.** lavishly

5. The use of such things as logos and color . . . . helps to maintain a
   corporate identity.
   a. schemes   **b.** systems   **c.** styles   **d.** fashions

6. We need to liaise more with politicians and the . . . . media if we want
   the government to agree to our plans.
   a. official   **b.** daily   **c.** mass   **d.** multi

7. $200,000 was . . . . for the grand opening of the new store.
   a. set aside   **b.** brought about   **c.** set off   **d.** laid up

8. Sponsorship can be an effective way of promoting . . . . towards an
   organization.
   a. will   **b.** goodwill   **c.** willingness   **d.** goodness

9. At a press reception don't . . . . guests with irrelevant material.
   a. overload   **b.** override   **c.** overtake   **d.** overcompensate

10. The reception must be held at a convenient . . . . with good
    transportation and parking facilities.
    a. revue   **b.** venue   **c.** view   **d.** venture

11. When making a presentation to a relatively small . . . . an overhead
    projector can be invaluable.
    a. assistance   **b.** spectator   **c.** audience   **d.** congregation

12. Within a large organization a well-designed . . . . journal is an effective
    method of internal communication.
    a. in-house   **b.** home   **c.** household   **d.** plant

13. Participating in local events, such as carnivals, is a good way of developing
    . . . . relations.
    a. common   **b.** commonplace   **c.** communal   **d.** community

14. We used every . . . . of communication to get our message across.
    a. style   **b.** approach   **c.** means   **d.** strategy

15. We have to highlight our strengths and . . . . any weaknesses.
    a. play up   **b.** think through   **c.** play down   **d.** talk back

31 Letters – 5 Sales

Below you will see extracts from three sales letters. Put the correct word or phrase in each blank. Choose from the following list. Use each item once only.

colleagues	featured	complimentary copy	recent publications
confident	needs	extensively tested	representatives
convenience	recommend	favorable response	specially selected
eligible	suitable	further information	subscription form
experience	value	highly popular	payment terms

A.

It is our pleasure to enclose a **1.** . . . . of one of our most **2.** . . . . ,
'American Business Vocabulary'.
You will notice that the book has a similar format to our **3.** . . . . series,
'American Vocabulary Program', but concentrates on vocabulary useful to
anyone who needs English in a business situation.
The exercises have been **4.** . . . . and have met with a **5.** . . . . from
both learners and teachers. The book is **6.** . . . . for use in the classroom
or for self-study.
We feel confident that you will want to **7.** . . . . this book to your
colleagues and students.

B.

We are a company with over 30 years **8.** . . . . in selling office equipment.
We have recently come out with a new selection of equipment and furniture
designed to meet the **9.** . . . . of today's electronic office.
This new selection is **10.** . . . . in our latest brochure which I have enclosed
together with details of our flexible **11.** . . . .
If you require any **12.** . . . . , simply telephone me and I will arrange for one
of our **13.** . . . . to get in touch with you at your convenience.

C.

You have been **14.** . . . . by my company to receive a free copy of
our latest publication 'Business Dealings'.
We cannot of course send a free copy to everyone but we have chosen
you because we **15.** . . . . your opinion. We are **16.** . . . . that you
will find it fascinating and want to show it to your **17.** . . . .
'Business Dealings' is published monthly and we have enclosed a
18. . . . . for your **19.** . . . . Subscribe within the next three
weeks and you will be **20.** . . . . for a discount of twenty per cent.

32 Advertising – 1

In advertising, the right choice of words can help to sell a product. If possible, look at some advertisements in English and see how many word partnerships you can find which create a favorable impression of the product.

Match each word on the left with a word on the right. Use each word once only. Write your answers in the boxes.

Set 1

1. competitive	a. brochure		1
2. delicious	b. cleaning		2
3. effortless	c. details		3
4. finest	d. fit		4
5. full	e. flavors		5
6. glossy	f. quality		6
7. perfect	g. rates		7
8. wide	h. variety		8

Set 2

Now do the same with these words.

1. fast-growing	a. brochure		1
2. full-color	b. company		2
3. multi-media	c. driving		3
4. highly-trained	d. recipes		4
5. money-saving	e. computer		5
6. mouth-watering	f. spray		6
7. ozone-friendly	g. staff		7
8. stress-free	h. tips		8

Now complete each sentence by using an expression from above.

1. Inside each stove there's a free cookbook full of . . . .

2. Our . . . . are ready to take care of your every need.

3. With hand-made shoes you get a . . . . every time.

4. The sophisticated power steering means . . . .

33 Opposites – 2

You can often build your vocabulary by asking yourself if you know the opposite of one of the most important words in a sentence.

It also helps to learn words in a complete sentence. This makes them easier to remember.

Complete each sentence with the opposite of the word in parentheses. Choose from the following list. Use each word once only. You must use the correct form of the verb.

accept	demolish	increase	reject
agree	expand	keep	strengthen
attack	gain	lose	succeed
complicate	impose	lower	withdraw

1. He's . . . . my recommendation. (ACCEPTED)

2. They're . . . . an office building down by the river. (CONSTRUCTING)

3. She . . . . the company's policy on the environment. (DEFENDED)

4. She went to the bank to . . . . some money. (DEPOSIT)

5. Is he the kind of person to . . . . his responsibilities? (AVOID)

6. I think his reorganization plan will ultimately . . . . (FAIL)

7. They've . . . . restrictions on using the fax. (LIFTED)

8. Share prices . . . . ground throughout the day. (LOST)

9. We . . . . a lot of money on that last deal. (MADE)

10. Did he . . . . his appointment with that journalist? (MISS)

11. They say the banks are going to . . . . interest rates. (RAISE)

12. I think this move will . . . . the deficit. (REDUCE)

13. Won't the new punching-in system . . . . things? (SIMPLIFY)

14. Getting outside finance can only . . . . our position. (WEAKEN)

15. Ship-building has . . . . in this area over the years. (DECLINED)

16. He . . . . that the company was in trouble. (DENIED)

34 Word formation – 2

Complete each sentence with the correct form of the word in capital letters. In some cases you will have to make a negative by using the prefix **il-**, **mis-** or **un-**.

1. EMPLOY

In an area of high . . . . people are desperate to find jobs.

Every . . . . of the firm is entitled to a 10% discount.

Her . . . . gets very angry if she uses the phone too much.

I'm looking for temporary . . . . during the summer vacation.

2. EXPENSE

It's . . . . to send the goods by air but they're needed urgently.

They offered her $15,000 plus . . . .

Unfortunately, ... on the project were much more than expected.

His . . . . claims are being looked at by the Chief Accountant.

3. EXPLAIN

If you read the . . . . leaflet, everything should become clear.

We're waiting for an . . . . of his behavior in the meeting.

4. EXTEND

We've decided to agree to their request for . . . . credit.

Could I speak to Miss Charles, please? I think it's . . . . 272.

The factory was . . . . damaged in the fire.

To some . . . . I agree with her conclusions.

5. FINANCE

Her . . . . adviser is convinced the project will be a success.

If the company is . . . . sound we might consider taking it over.

6. GROW

There is a . . . . awareness of the need to improve productivity.

The government is worried about the . . . . in consumer spending.

7. IMPRESS

It's important to make a good . . . . when meeting clients.

The results from our new Mexican subsidiary are very . . . .

I'm afraid she was . . . . by our presentation.

8. INDUSTRY

In this high-tech world, ... espionage is on the increase.

Mr Fredericks, a prominent . . . . , will head the investigating committee.

In some of the more . . . . countries pollution is a big problem.

9. INFLATE

I have no intention of paying such . . . . prices!

At the moment . . . . is running at 20%.

The government must take steps to halt the . . . . spiral.

10. INFORM

Please let me know if you need any more . . . .

I enjoyed her talk. It was very . . . .

I'm afraid you've been . . . . She no longer works for us.

11. INSTRUCT

The boss has left . . . . that she's not to be disturbed.

I can't make heads or tails of this . . . . manual!

12. INTRODUCE

The chairperson made some . . . . remarks and then she gave her talk.

I'd like to welcome Jane Phipps, who, I'm sure, needs no . . . .

13. INVEST

These shares have given me a good return on my . . . .

Small . . . . were advised to hold on to their shares.

14. KNOW

We need somebody with a good working . . . . of French.

Our company is virtually . . . . abroad.

She's obviously very . . . . as far as marketing is concerned.

15. LEGAL

It's . . . . to sell such goods without a proper permit.

They questioned the . . . . of the company's action.

35 Formal English

In some business letters and legal documents – more formal English is used. For example, although somebody might say:

We're trying to find out where she is.

in formal English this might be written as:

We are endeavoring to ascertain her whereabouts.

This is a rather extreme example as there has been a reaction against this type of language. However, it's still important to recognize this kind of formal language and to know its less formal equivalent.

Complete each sentence by using each word from the following list. At the end of each sentence write its less formal equivalent. Make sure you use the correct form of the verb.

anticipate	**facilitate**	**require**
comprehend	**perceive**	**terminate**
elapse	**purchase**	**possess**

1. He went into the jewellery store to . . . . a brooch for his wife.
    (. . . . .)

2. After talking to staff we can . . . . a need for a more efficient method of communicating decisions to the workforce. (. . . . .)

3. A week . . . . before he contacted them again. (. . . . .)

4. Things should be easier now. The law they passed should . . . . the setting up of small businesses. (. . . . .)

5. We'll . . . . more funding if this operation is to succeed. (. . . . .)

6. If deliveries don't improve, we'll be obliged to . . . . the contract.
    (. . . . .)

7. We do not . . . . any problems at this stage. (. . . . .)

8. We . . . . .several assets and securities. (. . . . .)

9. We feel that the directors have completely failed to . . . . how unsuitable the site is. (. . . . .)

36 Special areas – 3 Investing

Choose the best alternative to complete each sentence.

1. If a company needs to raise a lot of money, it may . . . . shares.
   a. put up   **b.** issue   **c.** supply   **d.** purchase
2. Mutual . . . . play an important role in the stock market.
   a. companies   **b.** trusts   **c.** societies   **d.** funds
3. As an ordinary shareholder, you are . . . . to vote at the meeting.
   a. entitled   **b.** titled   **c.** nominated   **d.** persuaded
4. The market . . . ., which is made up of a cross-section of shares, reflects the general activity of the market.
   a. indication   **b.** index   **c.** measure   **d.** indicator
5. A stock market condition in which the majority of stock prices are rising is a . . . . market.
   a. bear   **b.** bull   **c.** dog   **d.** cow
6. If the majority of stock prices are falling, it's called a . . . . market.
   a. bear   **b.** bull   **c.** dog   **d.** cow
7. A product which makes money simply by being on the market without much advertising is called a cash . . . .
   a. bear   **b.** bull   **c.** dog   **d.** cow
8. I've put part of the money into an instant . . . . account.
   a. access   **b.** excess   **c.** exit   **d.** entrance
9. Bonds issued by the government are often known as treasury . . . .
   a. receipts   **b.** statements   **c.** bills   **d.** debits
10. What kind of . . . . can I expect on my investment?
    a. reward   **b.** prize   **c.** surplus   **d.** return
11. You should have as diversified a . . . . of investments as possible.
    a. case   **b.** file   **c.** portfolio   **d.** folder
12. In real . . . ., the $1,000 you invested would be worth $5,000 today.
    a. words   **b.** facts   **c.** factors   **d.** terms
13. The higher the risk you . . . ., the more money you could make.
    a. take   **b.** do   **c.** make   **d.** invest
14. The market has been extremely . . . . over the past few years.
    a. volatile   **b.** wavering   **c.** shocking   **d.** moving

A s you did the exercise, did you make a note of these partnerships?
   stock market   **a return on an investment**
Look through the sentences again and underline any other word partnerships you find.

37 Social English – 2

Complete each of these conversations with an appropriate response from the list below. Use each response once only.

a. I don't think so.

b. Yes. As a matter of fact, it's my hobby.

c. Reception's as good a place as any.

d. Just a fruit juice, please.

e. Yes we must. I'll look forward to it.

f. I'm afraid not. It was fully booked.

g. Oh you shouldn't have! Thank you!

h. You're welcome.

i. It's difficult to say at this stage.

j. Oh, that's alright.

k. Not at all. Go ahead.

l. Do you think you could make it a little earlier?

1. . . . .

2. . . . .

3. . . . .

4. . . . .

5. . . . .

6. . . . .

7. . . . .

8. . . . .

9. . . . .

10. . . . .

11. . . . .

12. . . . .

38 Applying for a job

If you have an opportunity to read job advertisements (or the 'Want Ads') in English, use them to build your vocabulary. Notice especially how certain words and phrases keep recurring. You can also find information about the kinds of things people are expected to do in the jobs advertised.

A.

Below you will see some extracts from want ads. Fill in each blank with a word or phrase from the following list. Use each item once only.

competitive	initiative	suit	kitchen staff
ability	outgoing	team	pension plan
clear	preference	willing	potential customers
contact	required	busy office	successful candidate
experience	skills	hard work	thorough training

Our new 200-seat restaurant is opening in May and we are looking for waiters, waitresses and **1.** . . . .

If you are a friendly and **2.** . . . . person who is not afraid of **3.** . . . . , we have the job and hours to **4.** . . . . you.

For more information, **5.** . . . . Helen at (415) 331–2012.

Secretary/Receptionist **6.** . . . . for a **7.** . . . . Typing and shorthand between 80 and 120 wpm. We will give **8.** . . . . to applicants who have experience using word processors and computers.

TELEMARKETING PROFESSIONAL

We want a positive person who is **9.** . . . . to work hard and can use their own **10.** . . . . You must be lively and have a good sense of humor and a **11.** . . . . speaking voice.

You will receive **12.** . . . . to enable you to inform **13.** . . . . of the benefits of advertising with us.

Send resume to:

ADMINISTRATIVE CLERK

The **14.** . . . . will have had **15.** . . . . in bookkeeping and banking procedures.

The position calls for word-processing and secretarial **16.** . . . . plus the **17.** . . . . to work as part of a **18.** . . . .

A **19.** . . . . salary is offered as well as a company **20.** . . . .

B.

Now you will see extracts from two letters about the advertisement for administrative clerk.
Fill in each blank with a word from the following list. Use each word once only.

as	enclose	form	position
audio	inquiries	further	take
available	favorably	in	to
consider	for	opportunity	with

Dear Sir or Madam

In reference **1**......... your advertisement in today's 'Morning News', I am interested **2**......... applying for the **3**......... of administrative clerk with your company.

Could you please send me **4**......... details and an application **5**......... .

Sincerely

Dear Sir

I would like to apply **6**......... the position of administrative clerk with your company.

I **7**......... my application form.

I am presently working **8**......... a secretary in the accounts office at TW Industries. My responsibilities include **9**......... and copy typing and dealing **10**......... correspondence and telephone **11**......... .

Twice a week I have been going to evening classes in bookkeeping and I intend to **12**......... an examination in three months.

I am applying for the position because I would like an **13**......... to make more use of my training.

I would be **14**......... for an interview at any time.

I hope that you will **15**......... my application **16**......... .

Sincerely

39 Past tense – 2

Remember to check if a verb is irregular when you learn a new one. Remember also that some verbs that end in -ed in their past form have changes in their spelling, for example:

   try   tried   stop   stopped

Complete each of the sentences by using the past form of one of the verbs on the left and combining it with one of the words on the right. Use each verb once only. Some words on the left are used more than once.

write	give	rely	stick		back	off	over
carry	lay	run	stop		down	on	to
cut	leave	set			in	out	up
draw	pay	stand					

1. We . . . . of computer paper and we had to order some more.

2. They . . . . a survey on biological detergents.

3. He was bankrupt but he . . . . a company in his wife's name.

4. I . . . . for Claire while she was away at the conference.

5. The company needs to . . . . on unnecessary expenditures.

6. On the way to Australia I . . . . in Bangkok for two days.

7. They . . . . an agreement which satisfied both sides.

8. The hotels in Buenos Aires weren't cheap, but he . . . . the trip as a business expense for tax purposes.

9. Unfortunately we . . . . a supplier who was not able to supply us with the components he had promised.

10. They . . . . to consumer pressure and redesigned the package.

11. In his speech he . . . . the most important detail. How much is it all going to cost?

12. Last year Firmin's . . . . half their workforce because of the lack of orders.

13. He . . . . his original demand. We couldn't get him to change his mind.

14. They . . . . the money they had borrowed only after we had threatened to take them to court.

40 Special areas – 4 Accounting

Choose the best alternative to complete the sentence.

1. It's up to the accountant to . . . . the various financial statements.
   a. interpret **b.** intercept **c.** invent **d.** translate

2. The bookkeeper keeps a record of every financial . . . .
   a. action **b.** transaction **c.** entry **d.** transcription

3. It's essential to . . . . the invoice number in any correspondence.
   a. estimate **b.** quote **c.** say **d.** tell

4. The . . . . of the invoice goes to the customer, another copy goes to Sales, and we keep the other one here in Accounts.
   a. photocopy **b.** issue **c.** top copy **d.** account

5. We're in . . . . with our supplier over this invoice so don't pay it until you hear from me.
   a. argument **b.** dispute **c.** agreement **d.** distress

6. We send a . . . . to customers who haven't settled their accounts.
   a. reminder **b.** remainder **c.** remembrance **d.** memory

7. If these figures could be . . . . into parts and labor it would make them easier to understand.
   a. set up **b.** broken down **c.** rounded up **d.** laid down

8. This company has a weekly . . . . of about $100,000.
   a. pay **b.** payroll **c.** salary **d.** wage

9. Buying that new machinery has seriously . . . . our reserves.
   a. depreciated **b.** depleted **c.** depressed **d.** deprived

10. By examining the balance . . . . and other documents we were able to find out that the company was not doing as well as they claimed.
    a. slip **b.** ledger **c.** account **d.** sheet

11. We should be careful in our bookkeeping if we don't want to be . . . . by the government.
    a. audited **b.** audio **c.** inquired **d.** succeeded

12. The rent for the office is already 3 months . . . . !
    a. overtime **b.** in the red **c.** in demand **d.** overdue

13. Due to the economic climate we have had to . . . . more bad debts this year than ever before.
    a. tell off **b.** write off **c.** find out **d.** note down

14. Do they have enough working . . . . to keep trading?
    a. capital **b.** expenses **c.** accounts **d.** currency

15. Such items as buildings and machinery are known as . . . . assets.
    a. current **b.** hidden **c.** fixed **d.** liquid

41 Important adjectives

Spelling is often a problem in English. It's a good idea to make lists of words you find difficult to spell and test yourself regularly on them.
When you have done the exercise below, make two lists with the words and see how many more examples you can think of.

Is an 'a' or an 'e' missing from the following words?

confid nt	depend nt	perman nt
consist nt	domin nt	reluct nt
const nt	effici nt	excell nt
conveni nt	extravag nt	relev nt
curr nt	insolv nt	signific nt

Now complete the following sentences by using one of the adjectives above. Use each adjective once only.

1. I'm . . . . that we'll reach our target without any difficulty.

2. You should be familiar with the regulations . . . . to your work.

3. We must process these orders in a more . . . . way.

4. Unfortunately, the accounts show the company is . . . .

5. Short-term measures aren't enough. We need a more . . . . solution.

6. The advertising campaign had a . . . . effect on their sales.

7. I thought the use of computer graphics was an . . . . idea for your presentation.

8. You couldn't get a more . . . . location than next to the station!

9. The figures need . . . . updating as we get more information.

10. I hope interest rates don't stay at the . . . . level much longer!

11. The company fell unexpectedly from its . . . . market position.

12. I wish they had a more . . . . policy on discounts. You never know where you stand with them!

13. It was . . . . to spend so much on the press reception.

14. He's . . . . to invest any more money at the moment.

15. We are . . . . on overseas suppliers for most of our components.

42 Word partnerships – 4

Match each adjective on the left with a noun on the right to form common partnerships. Use each word once only. Write your answers in the boxes.

Set 1

1.	continuous	**a.**	aid	
2.	fundamental	**b.**	brochure	
3.	illustrated	**c.**	control	
4.	multi-national	**d.**	company	
5.	potential	**e.**	customer	
6.	prompt	**f.**	disagreement	
7.	strict	**g.**	reply	
8.	visual	**h.**	supply	

1	
2	
3	
4	
5	
6	
7	
8	

Set 2

Now do the same with these words.

1.	advanced	**a.**	arrangements	
2.	alternative	**b.**	attention	
3.	close	**c.**	expense	
4.	high	**d.**	labor	
5.	considerable	**e.**	materials	
6.	essential	**f.**	yield	
7.	manual	**g.**	requirement	
8.	raw	**h.**	technology	

1	
2	
3	
4	
5	
6	
7	
8	

Now complete each sentence using a suitable expression from above.

1. We can't use the hall so we'll have to make . . . .

2. They were recently taken over by a . . . .

3. I'd like you to meet her. She could be a . . . .

4. I want you to pay . . . . to everything he does.

43 Special areas – 5 Labor relations

Choose the best alternative to complete each sentence.

1. Where there was a closed . . . . agreement an employer could not hire non-union workers.
    a. shop   **b.** work   **c.** factory   **d.** business

2. Talks must take place within the . . . . of the national agreement.
    a. network   **b.** contest   **c.** framework   **d.** working party

3. We feel that salaries should at least keep . . . . with inflation.
    a. step   **b.** still   **c.** place   **d.** pace

4. They proposed to minimize lay-offs by offering an early . . . . plan option.
    a. retirement   **b.** retiring   **c.** age   **d.** leaving

5. With . . . . bargaining the unions negotiate on behalf of groups of workers, not individuals.
    a. collected   **b.** collection   **c.** collective   **d.** collecting

6. Depending on the result of the ballot, they may . . . . a strike.
    a. name   **b.** call   **c.** make   **d.** do

7. If they work to . . . . , the job might not be completed on time.
    a. rule   **b.** order   **c.** rules   **d.** regulation

8. The increase will be . . . . on employees agreeing to an operation to improve productivity.
    a. linked   **b.** connected   **c.** dependent   **d.** joined

9. Union members were asked not to cross the . . . . line.
    a. boycott   **b.** strike   **c.** picket   **d.** boundary

10. The union seemed powerless to stop the . . . . strikes.
    a. wildcat   **b.** mad dog   **c.** bald eagle   **d.** mad bull

11. The employers tried a . . . . to force the staff to accept their terms.
    a. lock-up   **b.** markup   **c.** lockout   **d.** knock-down

12. We've decided to recommend a half-day . . . . strike in support of our claim.
    a. voucher   **b.** token   **c.** backing   **d.** symbol

13. As we agreed to . . . . arbitration, we'll have to accept the decision.
    a. voluntary   **b.** free   **c.** binding   **d.** party

14. They voted to . . . . and try to prevent the factory from closing.
    a. set out   **b.** sit out   **c.** sit in   **d.** set up

15. As the unions have concentrated on the lower-paid workers in previous negotiations, ... have been eroded.
    a. differences   **b.** definitions   **c.** demonstrations   **d.** differentials

44 In the office – 2

Can you name all the items below? Use each of these words once only.

calculator   paper clips   scale   staples
date stamp   pencil sharpener   scissors   adding machine
guillotine   hole punch   stamps   tray
note pad   ruler   stapler   wastebasket

1. . . . .
2. . . . .
3. . . . .
4. . . . .

5. . . . .
6. . . . .
7. . . . .
8. . . . .

9. . . . .
10. . . . .
11. . . . .
12. . . . .

13. . . . .
14. . . . .
15. . . . .
16. . . . .

Now look at the page for one minute and then cover it. See how many items you can remember.

45 Noun and preposition

Combine a noun from the list on the left with a preposition from the list on the right to complete each sentence. You must use each noun once only, but each preposition can be used more than once.

access	congratulations	increase	result		
admiration	effect	intention	solution	**for**	**in**
chance	emphasis	interest		**of**	**on** **to**
confidence	experience	point			

1. He was full of . . . . the way she had chaired the meeting.

2. The rise in interest rates has had a considerable . . . . sales of furniture and kitchen appliances.

3. By taking them over we will gain . . . . new markets.

4. We have every . . . . your organizing ability.

5. I hope they find a . . . . this storage problem soon!

6. To cater to the growing . . . . information technology, we have had to add three extra courses this year.

7. Is there any . . . . seeing you about this some time today?

8. We need to put more . . . . improving staff morale rather than buying more equipment.

9. Have you had any . . . . this type of work?

10. There seemed to be no . . . . continuing the discussion.

11. They have been offered a considerable . . . . salary in return for more flexibility.

12. I have no . . . . resigning. It's up to them to dismiss me if they aren't satisfied.

13. By the way, ... winning the Waverley contract!

14. As a . . . . the adverse publicity, their sales went down.

How many of the expressions are followed by the **-ing** form of the verb? Look through the sentences again and underline the **-ing** forms. The examples on this page show again the importance of word partnerships.

---

46 Two-word expressions – 2

Join one word on the left with one from the right to make a two-word
partnership. Use each word once only. Write your answers in the boxes.

1. application	**a.**	bid		**1**	
2. assembly	**b.**	incentive		**2**	
3. balance	**c.**	book		**3**	
4. check	**d.**	buyout		**4**	
5. consumer	**e.**	chart		**5**	
6. feasibility	**f.**	control		**6**	
7. growth	**g.**	form		**7**	
8. business	**h.**	issue		**8**	
9. management	**i.**	line		**9**	
10. market	**j.**	potential		**10**	
11. pie	**k.**	protection		**11**	
12. bonus	**l.**	research		**12**	
13. quality	**m.**	scale		**13**	
14. salary	**n.**	sheet		**14**	
15. share	**o.**	card		**15**	
16. takeover	**p.**	study		**16**	

Now complete each sentence with one of the expressions.

1. If you produce above this amount, you get a . . . .

2. Working on this . . . . every day is very monotonous.

3. A big multi-national has made a . . . . for our company.

4. We carried out extensive . . . . before launching the product.

5. He's at the bottom of the . . . . so how can he afford it?

6. According to the . . . . , they made a large profit last year.

61

47 What's the job?

In this exercise you will see extracts from job advertisements.

You must decide which job is being referred to in each case.

Choose the job from the following list.

Each job is referred to once only.

Be careful because some of the jobs are looking for similar qualities from applicants.

accountant
advertising executive
assembly person
chauffeur

clerk
computer operator
draughtsperson
auto mechanic

personnel officer
R&D Manager
receptionist
sales representative

You will be in charge of a team of highly creative individuals delivering new quality products and enhancing our existing selection.

1. . . . .

With main responsibilities for hiring and selection. Communication skills and a pragmatic approach to problem solving essential.

2. . . . .

With mechanical design experience to work as a member of a team producing designs and drawings for production. Experience of our product selection is not essential.

3. . . . .

Duties include filing, mailing, relief reception and other general office work.

4. . . . .

Needed for night shift. Clean modern factory. Varied work. Good eyesight essential.

5. . . . .

Successful applicant will be articulate and presentable. Remuneration includes retainer and car allowance plus commission.

6. . . . .

Reporting directly to the President. You will take over financial control for all aspects of daily operation.

7. . . . .

Sober habits, clean driver's license, able to be on call 7 days per week at times. Uniform supplied.

8. . . . .

Must be experienced in the repair and maintenance of heavy duty vehicles. References must be provided from previous employers.

9. . . . .

You are the first person our clients will see so you need to be friendly, stylish and efficient.

10. . . . .

Some experience in the above-mentioned software is essential but training will be given to the successful applicant.

11. . . . .

You will be an essential member of an agency responsible for some of the country's top accounts. You will be responsible for the administration of local and national promotions.

12. . . . .

A s you were reading the advertisements, did you notice word partnerships such as *financial control* and *communication skills* ?
Look through the advertisements again and see how many more you can find.

Complete each of the sentences below with a suitable word partnership taken from the advertisements.

1. We're looking for new products to add to our . . . .

2. She's an . . . . of this team. We can't do without her.

3. You get more money if you work on the . . . . but it ruins your social life.

4. He had a very . . . . to solving problems.

5. I didn't get the job as a driver as I didn't have a . . . .

6. My . . . . are health and safety but I'm also concerned with the general welfare of employees.

48 Special areas – 6 Insurance

Choose the best alternative to complete each sentence.

1. Insurance companies can be considered as professional . . . . takers.
   a. life   **b.** risk   **c.** chance   **d.** misfortune

2. Some of the language in insurance . . . . is incomprehensible to most ordinary people.
   a. premiums   **b.** policies   **c.** rates   **d.** invoices

3. The company will . . . . the policy-holder against loss of or damage to the insured vehicle.
   a. identify   **b.** respect   **c.** indemnify   **d.** engage

4. Insurance companies like you to . . . . your claim as soon as possible.
   a. process   **b.** submit   **c.** assure   **d.** proceed

5. Go to an insurance . . . . and see if you can get a better deal.
   a. regent   **b.** agent   **c.** speculator   **d.** merchant

6. In these inflationary times it is important to keep the value of your policy closely . . . . to the value of your property.
   a. adapted   **b.** linked   **c.** indicated   **d.** dependent

7. My insurance company offers a wide . . . . of coverage.
   a. selection   **b.** branch   **c.** rank   **d.** standard

8. His insurance company had told him not to admit . . . . , even though it was clearly his fault.
   a. legality   **b.** likelihood   **c.** liability   **d.** crime

9. My endowment policy will . . . . when I'm sixty-five.
   a. ripen   **b.** mature   **c.** flourish   **d.** break

10. Natural . . . . insurance is obligatory in areas prone to floods, earthquakes, and hurricanes.
    a. damage   **b.** chaos   **c.** catastrophe   **d.** disaster

11. The money that the insured party must pay on any claim is called a . . . .
    a. deduction   **b.** debit   **c.** debt   **d.** deductible

12. The insurance will be . . . . if you omit any relevant information.
    a. void   **b.** valid   **c.** invaluable   **d.** priceless

13. You're allowed 30 days' . . . . period for the payment of the renewal premium.
    a. grace   **b.** favor   **c.** way   **d.** permission

14. Make sure all this equipment is insured . . . . accidental damage.
    a. over   **b.** against   **c.** with   **d.** from

49 Expressions with 'take'

Complete each sentence with the correct form of 'take' and a word from the list below. Use each word once only.

call	down	on	seriously
chair	further	out	steps
charge	home	over	notes
consideration	off	risk	

1. You should . . . . an additional policy covering you against accidental damage.

2. We had to . . . . extra staff during the holiday season.

3. When all the transportation costs have been . . . . into . . . . , we have in fact made a loss.

4. Sales really . . . . after the product had been mentioned on television.

5. A good sales rep can . . . . over $1000 a week.

6. If my phone rings, could you . . . . the . . . . for me?

7. We must . . . . to see that we don't lose our market share as a result of this increased competition.

8. If the boss is sick, who'll . . . . the . . . . at the meeting?

9. He didn't seem to . . . . the threat of unemployment very . . . .

10. Don't . . . . this . . . . , Steve. I'm just thinking aloud.

11. In 1988 we were . . . . by a large multi-national company.

12. If the account is not settled within seven days, we shall be obliged to . . . . the matter . . . .

13. Mrs Jenkins has been appointed to . . . . of our Florida branch.

14. I'm not sure if there is a market for this kind of product but you don't get anywhere without . . . . a . . . . now and again.

15. While the guest speaker delivered her speech, the audience . . . .

N otice once again how important word partnerships are. Underline all the expressions using 'take' and other words.

---

50 Business Jargon

Understanding the jargon of business English is very important. Use the following common phrases to complete the sentences, using the correct verb form where necessary:

number-crunching	break even
take a nose dive	through the grapevine
sell like hotcakes	go belly-up
fall by the wayside	politically correct
head-to-head	a niche
market globalization	go public
word-of-mouth	on the cutting edge

1. The new multi-media computer failed in Europe, but is . . . . in the Asian market.

2. We don't bother advertising heavily in the media since most of our business comes from . . . . advertising.

3. RHF Enterprises had incredible success in the 80's until they . . . . just last year.

4. The new 2-door sports coupe is designed to go . . . . with the competition's existing model of similar design.

5. Our chain of fitness centers has carved out . . . . in the fast-track executive market that previously had not existed.

6. Before we bring this product onto the market we need to do some more . . . . to be sure our calculations are accurate.

7. We should think about our overseas competitors now since the tendency in today's business environment is toward . . . .

8. They abandoned the company after two years of just . . . . , without showing profit nor loss.

9. The business is currently a privately-owned enterprise but they're considering . . . . and selling shares.

10. Our electronic products are always innovative and . . . . of today's technology.

11. In order not to offend any individuals or groups we should try to be . . . . in our advertising.

12. Stocks . . . . yesterday afternoon, falling 40 points to 3,648.

13. Inevitably many new products . . . . in the rush for profits.

14. They had heard . . . . that he was thinking of leaving.

51 Confusing words – 2

Choose the correct word for each sentence.

1. I'll ask my broker for **advice/ advise** on investment.

2. He first spoke **briefly/shortly** about the agenda for the day.

3. She hopes to get a **chair/seat** on the board.

4. We **check/control** each new consignment very carefully.

5. Expensive hotels often supply their guests with **complimentary/complementary** champagne.

6. Do these cars **confirm/conform** to the new safety regulations?

7. You shouldn't read **confident/confidential** documents!

8. Normally, she's a very **conscientious/conscious** worker.

9. The unions criticized the government's **economic/economical** policy.

10. If you pay too much tax you get a **discount/refund**.

11. Lawyers here only get their **fee/wages** if they win the case.

12. The **income/salary** from the investment is $52,000 a year.

13. In order to understand the potential of a product, much marketing **research/investigation** is necessary.

14. There's a lot of **competition/competence** in this industry.

15. The secretary took **notes/notices** of what was said at the meeting.

16. The **overtake/takeover** bid from Jenkins came as a complete surprise.

17. Please send me your latest catalog and **price/prize** list.

18. We've increased **produce/productivity** by 10% in this factory.

Now see if you can write a new, correct sentence using the incorrect word from each of these sentences. This will help you to remember how to use the words you have seen.

---

52 Word formation – 3

Remember to keep looking for words that are formed from the same basic word. Make lists of these words and test yourself. Try to use the words in sentences. This will help you to remember them.

Complete each sentence with the correct form of the word in capital letters. In some cases you will have to make a negative form by using the prefix **dis-** or **un-**.

1. MANAGE

Since the . . . . buy-out profits have risen sharply.

The General . . . . sent a letter to every member of staff.

It makes sense to break the task up into . . . . steps.

2. NEGOTIATE

The salary is . . . . so how much do you think I should ask for?

Unfortunately, ... with the union have broken down.

3. OCCUPY

The block has been . . . . since the fire.

Dust is an . . . . hazard in this factory.

4. OPERATE

The oil rig should be in . . . . by tomorrow morning.

We expect an . . . . profit of at least 20 million dollars next year.

The system should be fully . . . . by this time next year.

The switchboard . . . . was unable to find the person I wanted.

5. OPT

Although insurance is . . . . , we strongly recommend it.

I want to leave my . . . . open, so I haven't given him my answer yet.

6. ORIGIN

We . . . . intended to close only three of our branches.

The idea is said to have . . . . from the Sales Department.

Her proposal showed a lot of . . . . - perhaps too much, in fact.

7. PREFER

We'll obviously give . . . . to candidates with previous experience.

They gave her the loan at a . . . . rate of interest.

8. PRODUCE

The new model should be in . . . . in three months.
The finished . . . . must leave the factory in perfect condition.
I'm afraid our talks with the manufacturers have been . . . .
We hope that longer lunch hours will increase worker . . . .

9. PROFIT

Any line which proved . . . . was immediately discontinued.
Doubts have been expressed as to the . . . . of the business.

10. RESTRICT

They have imposed . . . . on the selling of certain electronic goods.
Such . . . . trade practices are not in the public interest.
I'm afraid access to this information is . . . .

11. SATISFY

What job . . . . can anybody get from working on an assembly line?
We hope the discussions with our creditors will have a . . . . outcome.
The customer was . . . . with the service and complained to the boss.

12. SYSTEM

You need to have a . . . . approach in this type of work.
We need to carry out this survey . . . .

13. SUIT

I'm not sure about the . . . . of the site for the new factory.
We now have to find a . . . . name for our new chocolate bar.

14. VARY

Our company produces a great . . . . of toys.
Remember the interest rate is . . . . , so you could have problems.
They put forward . . . . suggestions but none was acceptable.

O ften the words are used as parts of word partnerships, for example:

give preference   job satisfaction

Underline other useful partnerships you can find in the sentences.

---

53 Special areas – 7 International trade

Choose the best alternative to complete the sentence.

1. Many countries, such as the United Kingdom and New Zealand, are . . . . dependent on international trade.
   a. favorably   **b.** heavily   **c.** perfectly   **d.** grossly

2. The fact that labor costs are lower in other countries . . . . us at a tremendous disadvantage.
   a. makes   **b.** does   **c.** puts   **d.** sells

3. If a country has a . . . . currency, importers and exporters may have to keep changing the prices of their goods.
   a. swimming   **b.** flying   **c.** flowing   **d.** floating

4. Some countries try to be . . . . in certain commodities so that they are not dependent on imports.
   a. economic   **b.** sufficient   **c.** self-sufficient   **d.** self-financing

5. It's better to start exporting on a small . . . . and then expand if things go well.
   a. measure   **b.** measurement   **c.** scale   **d.** rate

6. Because of high shipping costs, it made more sense to . . . . a manufacturer to produce our selection of furniture.
   a. license   **b.** lease   **c.** control   **d.** handle

7. The government has imposed protective tariffs to stop the . . . . of cheap imports which threatened to destroy domestic industries.
   a. rain   **b.** famine   **c.** flood   **d.** storm

8. Some manufacturers were accused of . . . . , in other words selling goods abroad at a lower price than they were sold domestically.
   a. dumping   **b.** revaluing   **c.** flooding   **d.** devaluation

9. Employing more staff has reduced our . . . . time in the port.
   a. turning   **b.** turn-around   **c.** turn back   **d.** turnover

10. The technical . . . . for electrical equipment can vary from country to country.
    a. justification   **b.** rules   **c.** specifications   **d.** uniforms

11. Many goods coming here are subject . . . . customs duty.
    a. for   **b.** to   **c.** of   **d.** with

12. Among other things, a . . . . contains details of the goods, their destination and the name of the ship carrying them.
    a. bill of lading   **b.** way-bill   **c.** bill of exchange   **d.** receipt

13. The person the goods are sent to is called a . . . .
    a. consignor   **b.** consignee   **c.** commissioner   **d.** master

14. She looked at the . . . . to check where the goods were produced.
    a. certificate of origin   **b.** test certificate   **c.** postmark   **d.** trade mark

15. China, Hong Kong, Singapore, Malaysia, South Korea, and Thailand all compose countries belonging to the Pacific . . . . trade zone.
    a. Area   **b.** Wheel   **c.** Hub   **d.** Rim

54 Color idioms

Complete each sentence with the correct color.

1. Because we do business differently, we have always been considered the . . . . sheep of our business.

2. I must be . . . . -listed because I have a lot of difficulty getting credit.

3. We're waiting for the . . . . light from upstairs to launch our publicity campaign.

4. Aside from a few managers, employment at Target Auto is limited to mostly . . . . -collar jobs.

5. I won't believe we have the contract until I see it down in . . . . and . . . .

6. Marketers often refer to the senior citizen market as the . . . . market.

7. If I catch the eleven thirty . . . . -eye flight tonight, I can be in Houston by 8:00 tomorrow morning.

8. We need to cut through all the . . . . tape and speed up the decision-making process.

9. It's difficult to say who exactly is responsible for recruiting. It's kind of a . . . . area.

10. The company found itself several thousand dollars in the . . . . after spending so much on improving its production line.

11. My father always said a . . . . chip stock is always a good investment.

12. They're looking for a . . . . knight to help them fight the takeover bid.

13. Then, out of the . . . . , she offered me a job managing her new restaurant. You can imagine my surprise.

14. We have to roll out the . . . . carpet for him as he's one of our best customers.

15. The failure of last year's model is one of the biggest . . . . elephants we've every had.

16. The government intends to allocate more money to unemployment . . . . spots.

55 Adjective and preposition

Combine an adjective from the list on the left with a preposition from the list on the right to complete each sentence. You must use each adjective once only, but each preposition can be used more than once.

acceptable	capable	eligible	proud		
accustomed	consistent	envious	relevant	for	of
available	contrary	familiar	responsible	on	to with
aware	dependent	popular	well-known		

1. I'm sure they must be . . . . our products as they're used all over the world.

2. If you pay within seven days you will be . . . . a discount.

3. I will be . . . . an interview at any time.

4. The other salespeople were all . . . . her success and so they were pleased when she left.

5. . . . . expectations, our sales figures went down last month.

6. Our new selection of toys has proved very . . . . children who have watched the television show.

7. Any decisions made must be . . . . the company's overall marketing strategy.

8. The maintenance engineer is . . . . checking every machine at least once a week.

9. I'm not . . . . any regulations that should prevent us from exporting to those countries.

10. We need somebody who is . . . . understanding German.

11. That's an interesting point but it isn't really . . . . our discussion.

12. It took me some time to become . . . . using the new system.

13. They will only sign if the terms are fully . . . . them.

14. It's risky to be . . . . only one supplier.

15. He was so . . . . his firm's achievements that he talked about them to everyone he met.

16. This company is . . . . the high quality of its products.

56 Word partnerships – 5

Match each verb on the left with a noun on the right to form common
partnerships. Use each word once only. Write your answers in the boxes.

Set 1

1. attend	**a.** a compromise		1	
2. consult	**b.** a conference		2	
3. establish	**c.** an error		3	
4. issue	**d.** funds		4	
5. reach	**e.** instructions		5	
6. rectify	**f.** a lawyer		6	
7. set	**g.** priorities		7	
8. transfer	**h.** the pace		8	

Set 2

Now do the same with these words.

1. allocate	**a.** a deal		1	
2. break	**b.** a demand		2	
3. close	**c.** duty		3	
4. corner	**d.** figures		4	
5. meet	**e.** the market		5	
6. pay	**f.** new ground		6	
7. raise	**g.** standards		7	
8. update	**h.** tasks		8	

Now complete each sentence using a suitable expression from above.

1. The US and Japan still. . . . . . .for the laptop computer market.

2. I had to . . . . on those items when I came through customs.

3. If they're threatening to take you to court you'd better . . . .

4. How easy is it to . . . . to a bank in another country?

73

57 Special areas – 8 Personnel

Choose the best alternative to complete each sentence.

1. The personnel department . . . . a job analysis, which is a detailed study of the elements and characteristics of each job.
   a. carries on   **b.** carries out   **c.** goes on   **d.** goes through

2. They write a job description specifying the . . . . of the job.
   a. objects   **b.** objectives   **c.** results   **d.** characters

3. You should encourage employees . . . . openly about any problems.
   a. for speaking   **b.** to tell   **c.** to say   **d.** to speak.

4. The first step in the disciplinary procedure is an . . . . reprimand.
   a. aural   **b.** oral   **c.** open   **d.** overt

5. He doesn't seem to . . . . very well with the other secretaries.
   a. come on   **b.** get along   **c.** get by   **d.** get through

6. By organizing job . . . . you can give staff experience in many different departments.
   a. revolution   **b.** recycling   **c.** circulation   **d.** rotation

7. After . . . . our training program, we made some changes.
   a. evaluating   **b.** valuing   **c.** vindicating   **d.** validating

8. Our selection procedure is based on the old saying: "You can't fit a square . . . . into a round hole."
   a. bar   **b.** stick   **c.** wood   **d.** peg

9. Before you get the job you have to have a . . . . examination.
   a. medicine   **b.** mechanical   **c.** medical   **d.** medicinal

10. Training new staff is . . . . , so you must pick the right person.
    a. costly   **b.** priceless   **c.** valuable   **d.** cost-effective

11. We can't use . . . . titles such as 'mailman' and 'fireman'.
    a. sexual   **b.** sexy   **c.** sexist   **d.** sexism

12. We have a policy of . . . . our own employees first for any vacancies.
    a. thinking   **b.** considering   **c.** asking   **d.** telling

13. As part of the . . . . process, Personnel check each applicant's qualifications before considering them for an interview.
    a. monitoring   **b.** warning   **c.** screening   **d.** forecasting

14. Tests are used to measure the applicant's . . . . for the job.
    a. attitude   **b.** success   **c.** discrimination   **d.** aptitude

15. The personnel department helps to organize an . . . . program for each new employee.
    a. orientation   **b.** orienteering   **c.** inducement   **d.** endurance

16. If we have to dismiss an employee this means the . . . . process has failed in some way.
    a. selective   **b.** chosen   **c.** selection   **d.** choice

17. Highly-skilled jobs are usually advertised in the . . . . media, such as technical magazines.
    a. special   **b.** speciality   **c.** specialist   **d.** specialization

18. Using a standardized application form ensures we get all the . . . . we need.
    a. particulars   **b.** specialities   **c.** peculiarities   **d.** experience

19. One important aspect of employee relations is ensuring that there is no . . . . in the work place.
    a. discrepancy   **b.** harmony   **c.** discrimination   **d.** discretion

20. Some of the employees were not happy about the introduction of a yearly . . . . interview.
    a. approval   **b.** appraisal   **c.** appreciation   **d.** appropriation

21. Her work was beginning to suffer because of family . . . .
    a. committees   **b.** commissions   **c.** competition   **d.** commitments

22. After a time employees may feel they are . . . . with a job they find tedious.
    a. glued   **b.** stuck   **c.** fastened   **d.** attached

23. His work is generally satisfactory but unfortunately he has a . . . . against his supervisor.
    a. hatred   **b.** dissatisfaction   **c.** disagreement   **d.** grudge

24. "Why does the personnel director always . . . . me? I'm not the only one who comes late!"
    a. pick up   **b.** pick on   **c.** pick with   **d.** pick out

25. In cases of . . . . we sometimes make loans to employees.
    a. hard cash   **b.** hardship   **c.** hard labor   **d.** hard sell.

26. In R & D, for example, employing someone . . . . unorthodox may produce stimulating ideas.
    a. slightly   **b.** scarcely   **c.** lightly   **d.** hardly

27. A complete . . . . is kept on every senior member of staff from the moment they are appointed.
    a. document   **b.** paper   **c.** dossier   **d.** diary

28. Positive . . . . is essential so that staff know that their efforts are appreciated.
    a. feedback   **b.** discrimination   **c.** commentary   **d.** notification

58 Expressions with 'in'

Remember to keep looking for examples of words which combine together to form common expressions.

There are several expressions in English using prepositions. If you look up one of these expressions in a dictionary you will sometimes find it under the preposition. Often, however, you have to look under the noun.

Here are some expressions with 'in'. Make sure you understand them before doing the exercise.

in accordance with	in debt	in the process of
in advance	in due course	in charge of
in mind	in error	in stock
in circulation	in a position to	in transit

Put the correct expression from the above list into the following sentences. Use each expression once only.

1. We regret that we are not . . . . extend you any more credit.

2. We have sold your car . . . . your instructions.

3. The government wants to reduce the amount of money . . . .

4. He is heavily . . . . because he still hasn't been paid for the last job he did.

5. Management put me. . . . . the billing department.

6. You'll receive half the payment . . . . and the rest when the work has been completed.

7. We have over 500 carpets . . . . in our warehouse.

8. The goods were sent . . . . We apologize for any inconvenience this may have caused.

9. You should receive the information . . . . so please try and be patient.

10. They are . . . . installing a new computer-controlled system, so your order might be delayed.

11. We have no room on our staff for you right now, but we'll keep you . . . . for any future vacancies.

12. The goods were damaged . . . . from the factory to the warehouse.

59 Advertising – 2

Choose the best alternative to complete the sentence.
Look up any words you don't know.

1. With effective advertising a company can become a . . . . name.
    a. house   **b.** household   **c.** housewife's   **d.** home

2. We need an effective campaign to . . . . our new product line.
    a. fire   **b.** set out   **c.** set off   **d.** launch

3. During the commercial . . . ., there was an advertisement for a new women's magazine.
    a. break   **b.** breakage   **c.** pause   **d.** interval

4. The first thing an ad must do is . . . . the reader's eye.
    a. trap   **b.** catch   **c.** find   **d.** reach

5. We need a name for the product which will . . . . to teenagers.
    a. draw   **b.** attract   **c.** succeed   **d.** appeal

6. We need a new . . . . .that people can remember us by.
    a. slogan   **b.** sentence   **c.** phrase   **d.** lyric

7. All advertisers must obey the industry's . . . .
    a. practice code   **b.** code of practice   **c.** practical code   **d.** code word

8. Advertising on television is very expensive during . . . . viewing hours.
    a. peak   **b.** high   **c.** audience   **d.** big

9. We did a lot of research to ensure that the advertisement would appeal to the . . . . audience.
    a. aim   **b.** arrival   **c.** goal   **d.** target

10. Newspaper advertising . . . . for 45% of the total.
    a. accounted   **b.** counted   **c.** comprised   **d.** came

11. Advertisers look at each newspaper's . . . . figures before deciding where to place their advertisements.
    a. circular   **b.** population   **c.** circulation   **d.** revenue

12. As part of our service we provide . . . . display material.
    a. selling point   **b.** point-of-sale   **c.** appointed   **d.** salesmanship

13. If you advertise at airports, you have a . . . . audience.
    a. captured   **b.** slave   **c.** captivated   **d.** captive

14. She does the art work while I write the . . . . for each advertisement.
    a. copy   **b.** copies   **c.** copyright   **d.** media

60 Letters – 6
Exhibition information

Below you will see an extract from a letter giving information about a business exhibition. Fill in each blank by using a word or phrase from the list below. Use each item once only.

emphasis	enclosed map	company details	new feature
enter	pleased	complimentary tickets	ideal opportunity
field	look forward	comprehensive selection	in-depth discussion
speakers	up to date	conveniently situated	series of lectures

We are **1.**........to enclose two **2.**........for this year's Business Scene Exhibition.

As your business grows it is important to keep **3.**........with the latest developments. With over 400 exhibitors this year the Exhibition is bigger and better than ever. This is the **4.**........to see a **5.**........of the latest products, services and publications.

A **6.**........of the Exhibition this year is a **7.**........on international trade and investment. Distinguished **8.**........from around the world will give their views on the changes taking place. Special **9.**........will be given to the ever-increasing role of the new technologies especially in the **10.**........of international communications.

At the end of each lecture there will be opportunities for **11.**........of the issues raised.

As you will see from the **12.**........, the Exhibition takes place at a venue **13.**........only a 10 minute drive from the station.

The Exhibition is open from 10 a.m to 6 p.m. on 1st, 2nd and 3rd of May.

Simply **14.**........your names and **15.**........on the badges provided and bring your tickets to the business show of the year!

We **16.**........to seeing you there.

61 Word partnerships – 6

As you use English in business you meet several expressions using 'of', for example:

brand of soap   **exchange of contracts**

Can you think of any more?

In this exercise you must complete the expression on the left by using one of the words on the right. Use each word once only. Write your answer in the space provided.

1.	breach	of	absence
2.	code	of	charges
3.	rule	of	contract
4.	leave	of	thumb
5.	loss	of	earnings
6.	margin	of	embarkation
7.	word	of	error
8.	port	of	hands
9.	rate	of	living
10.	breakdown	of	mouth
11.	show	of	practice
12.	standard	of	return

Now complete the following by using an expression from above.

1. She looked for an investment with a better . . . .

2. It's not mandatory, but as a . . . ., you should always keep the length of your resumé to just one page.

3. They sued him for . . . . as the work was not completed on time.

4. The meeting approved the motion by a . . . .

5. In theory, public relations officers follow a strict . . . .

62 Social English – 3

Match the sentence on the left with a suitable response on the right. Use each sentence once only.

1. And what line of work are you in?

    a. No. This is my first visit, in fact.

2. I'm afraid I didn't bring the letter.

    b. At this time of day? Not very good, I'm afraid.

3. Best of luck on Friday.

    c. Smart move!

4. Should I get you a taxi?

    d. No, please. Lunch is on me.

5. How was the conference?

    e. Thanks! We'll need it!

6. What are the chances of finding him at home?

    f. Shall we say about eleven thirty, then?

7. Do you know Chicago at all, Wendy?

    g. I might. I'll look in my planner.

8. I've decided to look around for a better job.

    h. Public relations.

9. Thursday morning would suit me fine.

    i. Never mind. You can give it to me tomorrow.

10. You don't have his phone number by any chance?

    j. No, it's all right, thanks. The walk will do me good.

11. How's their recruiting drive going?

    k. Not too bad. I made some useful contacts.

12. I'll ask our waiter for the check.

    l. They've had quite a good response so far.

Write your answers here:

1	2	3	4	5	6	7	8	9	10	11	12

Can you think of any more responses you could give to the sentences on the left?

63 Special areas – 9 The law

Choose the best alternative to complete each sentence.

1. The company took out an . . . . to prevent the newspaper from publishing the story.
   a. incentive   **b.** injunction   **c.** inducement   **d.** induction

2. Every business must operate within the legal . . . . of the country.
   a. pattern   **b.** standard   **c.** framework   **d.** requirement

3. They have changed the wording on the package to . . . . the new regulations.
   a. comply with   **b.** come to   **c.** call up   **d.** take up

4. An employer is not allowed to discriminate . . . . an employee because of race or color.
   a. for   **b.** between   **c.** with   **d.** against

5. You realize that you will be . . . . for any debts incurred if you sign this agreement?
   a. likely   **b.** apt   **c.** liable   **d.** bound

6. If you fail to deliver on time you will be in . . . . of contract.
   a. break   **b.** failure   **c.** fault   **d.** breach

7. The company threatened to . . . . the newspaper for libel unless an immediate apology was published.
   a. court   **b.** sue   **c.** subject   **d.** slander

8. Until you can prove you have a legal . . . . to the property, we are not prepared to do business with you.
   a. claim   **b.** responsibility   **c.** action   **d.** status

9. As this is the first case of its kind it really depends on how the court . . . . the law.
   a. interprets   **b.** translates   **c.** explains   **d.** performs

10. They proved that the accident was the result of his . . . .
    a. negligent   **b.** responsibility   **c.** negligence   **d.** competence

11. They paid $1 million in . . . . because of those faulty components.
    a. damage   **b.** compensation   **c.** harm   **d.** errors

12. We can't use that name because it's a registered . . . .
    a. trademark   **b.** patent   **c.** logo   **d.** copyright

13. I think we should . . . . our lawyers before signing any agreement.
    a. confirm   **b.** contract   **c.** consign   **d.** consult

14. The new law will strengthen . . . . against unfair dismissal.
    a. safeguards   **b.** prevention   **c.** grants   **d.** avoidance

15. Litigation is on the . . . . as consumers become more conscious of their rights.
    a. surge   **b.** escalation   **c.** development   **d.** rise

64 Choose the adverb – 2

From the following list choose a suitable adverb to complete each sentence. Use each adverb once only.

absolutely	**firmly**	**instantaneously**	**unpredictably**
adversely	**formally**	**irretrievably**	**financially**
consistently	**highly**	**readily**	
convincingly	**initially**	**systematically**	

1. The change-over must be carried out . . . . , one step at a time.

2. Spare parts are . . . . available so there should be no problem.

3. We had no trouble raising the loan, since the banker was sure we were . . . . sound.

4. They have . . . . out-performed their competitors and we see no reason why this should change.

5. Moves are under way to . . . . shut down the company.

6. Are you . . . . certain the appointment was for midday?

7. I . . . . believe that this selection will be a winner.

8. Their latest figures demonstrate . . . . that their shares are ready for a big rise! Buy now!

9. I'm afraid talks with the unions have broken down . . . .

10. We've decided to concentrate . . . . on the South Pacific and then, if successful, try to get into other markets.

11. News of the loss could . . . . affect the share price.

12. Electronic mail systems allow you to reply . . . . to messages.

13. The general manager made a . . . . entertaining speech.

14. The markets tend to act . . . . in times of crisis.

N ow look for and underline the word partnerships containing these important adverbs.

---

65 Letters – 7
Booking a hotel room

Below you will see parts of two letters concerned with booking hotel rooms for a company. Put the correct word or phrase in each blank. Choose from the following list. Use each item once only.

available	meet	reasonable rates	suitable
brochure	pleasure	require	training sessions
full board	provide	requirements	urge
hesitate	quotation	single	without delay

A.

We intend to hold **1.** . . . . for our sales representatives at the end of May next year and are looking for a hotel which provides **2.** . . . . facilities.

Our **3.** . . . . are as follows:

    1 room for lectures capable of seating approximately 50 people

    5 smaller rooms for seminars capable of seating 10-12 people

    50-60 **4.** . . . . rooms

If you can **5.** . . . . these facilities, we would be pleased to receive your **6.** . . . . for 3 nights **7.** . . . . starting with dinner on Tuesday and finishing with lunch on Friday.

We look forward to hearing from you.

B.

Thank you for your letter of September 6th, inquiring about our conference facilities.

I have enclosed our **8.** . . . . and price list.

As you will see, we should be able to **9.** . . . . your requirements at what we consider to be very **10.** . . . .

At the moment our rooms are still **11.** . . . . for the end of May, but I would **12.** . . . . you to make your reservation **13.** . . . . as this is a popular time of the year with many companies.

If you **14.** . . . . any further information, please do not **15.** . . . . to contact me.

I hope that we will have the **16.** . . . . of welcoming you to our hotel.

66 Increasing efficiency

In what ways can an organization be made more efficient? Before you do this exercise see if you can write down in English at least 5 ways. As you read the text, see if any points are the same as yours.

Remember that predicting what somebody is going to say or write can help you to practice and build your vocabulary.

Fill each blank with the correct word partnership from the list below. Use each partnership once only.

put off unpleasant tasks	**lose concentration**	**separate folders**
delegate routine tasks	**set a time limit**	**set priorities**
unnecessary paperwork	**members of staff**	**skip over**
time-consuming way	**have a meeting**	**pick out**

Here are ten key ways to improve efficiency:

Avoid **1.** . . . . Be ruthless. Are all those statistics and memos really necessary?

Essential paperwork should be organized into **2.** . . . . so that you and other **3.** . . . . can find what you want quickly.

4. . . . . Decide which of your tasks are the most important and deal with them first.

Never **5.** . . . . It is best to deal with them as soon as possible or you will keep thinking about them and **6.** . . . .

Know when to stop. If you are too much of a perfectionist, you will concentrate on one task and not leave enough time to do the others.

7. . . . . Don't try to do everything yourself. Make sure, however, that the subordinate is competent enough to carry out the task.

Cut meetings to a minimum. Ask yourself if a meeting is essential or if the issues could be dealt with in a less **8.** . . . .

If you must **9.** . . . ., restrict it to those whose presence is essential. Don't waste people's time.

At the beginning of a meeting **10.** . . . . and stick to it. This should focus everbody's mind and avoid unnecessary anecdotes etc.

Learn the art of speed-reading. **11.** . . . . the non-essential text and **12.** . . . . the message, the important facts.

67 Special areas – 10 Management

Choose the best alternative to complete each sentence.

1. You must keep staff . . . . , especially when things get difficult.
   a. generated   **b.** motivated   **c.** frustrated   **d.** electrified

2. Weigh the . . . . of each alternative before deciding.
   a. checks and balances   **b.** assets   **c.** pros and cons   **d.** profits

3. A good manager must be able to handle . . . . situations.
   a. sensible   **b.** impressive   **c.** touching   **d.** touchy

4. He decided to let things . . . . , so he dropped the subject until later.
   a. freeze   **b.** ice over   **c.** cool down   **d.** flare up

5. A good staff needs to feel . . . . by management to take initiatives and contribute to the business.
   a. empowered   **b.** excited   **c.** exhausted   **d.** endowed

6. We need to have a . . . . plan in case things don't work out.
   a. container   **b.** contingency   **c.** consolidated   **d.** consecutive

7. A good manager knows when it's time to . . . . operations when business gets too big.
   a. downshift   **b.** shrink   **c.** downsize   **d.** halt

8. Why doesn't he stick to the point? He's always going off . . . .
   a. at an angle   **b.** on a tangent   **c.** by the way   **d.** on the side

9. It's always difficult when a team is working . . . . a deadline.
   a. in   **b.** at   **c.** to   **d.** opposite

10. Try to ensure that each employee's . . . . is not too great.
    a. workload   **b.** working practice   **c.** work-to-rule   **d.** working party

11. Those who can't manage their time efficiently always have high stress . . . .
    a. grades   **b.** standards   **c.** performances   **d.** levels

12. The more responsibilities she . . . . , the more mistakes she made.
    a. took off   **b.** took on   **c.** took down   **d.** took out

13. I hope the project continues to run as . . . . as it has so far.
    a. calmly   **b.** confidently   **c.** smoothly   **d.** wisely

14. After . . . . many unforeseen obstacles they just managed to meet their deadline.
    a. overtaking   **b.** overcoming   **c.** overwhelming   **d.** overriding

15. What can we do to improve . . . . in this department?
    a. morale   **b.** mortality   **c.** moral   **d.** temperament

As usual, look for and underline useful word partnerships.

68 Metaphors in Business – 2

Since sports in America play such an important role in everyday life, another significant metaphor in business English is the use of sports terms. When you watch a game or read the sports page in the newspaper in English, be aware of the language being used and then think if it can be used when talking about business – most likely it can!

Complete the sentences with the following phrases from the world of sport:

ballpark figure	**neck and neck**	**sales pitch**
by the rules	**play hardball**	**struck out**
heavyweights	**rain check**	**team work**
in the running	**rebound**	**touch base**
major player	**right off the bat**	**inside track**

1. Somehow our company was able to . . . . this year after taking hefty losses early last summer.

2. Sorry, I'm busy tomorrow evening. Can I take a . . . .

3. The trick to making a lot of sales is to have a quick . . . .

4. I don't have the exact cost estimate with me, but I can give you a . . . .

5. Be careful with those guys. They . . . . , and are not timid negotiators.

6. Although our company has gained a lot of market share, I don't believe we're ready to compete with the . . . . just yet.

7. Francisco Industries will be a . . . . in this market come next year.

8. Sandra's depressed today because she . . . . with that big client she was hoping to sign.

9. No, they didn't hesitate. They said 'no' . . . .

10. Corporation of the Year? No chance! We're not even . . . .

11. I wanted to . . . . with you earlier but your secretary said you were busy.

12. I don't mind a little competition as long as they play . . . . and don't do anything unethical.

13. Rent-and-Save and Frugal Rentals are . . . . right now and no one seems to want to take a lead in that market.

14. I'm afraid that the competition has the . . . . in Mexico since they were there before us and are familiar with that market.

15. Good work from individuals is important but the most productive work is always accomplished through . . . .

Test 1 – Units 1 – 14

Choose the best alternative to complete each example:

1. Success in business can depend on how . . . . a company is.
   a. competition   **b.** competitive   **c.** compatible   **d.** comparable

2. The accurate record of a meeting is the . . . .
   a. notes   **b.** jottings   **c.** minutes   **d.** hours

3. It is necessary before starting a business to . . . . sufficient capital.
   a. rise   **b.** grow   **c.** raise   **d.** arise

4. To sell more of a particular product, you may wish to offer a higher
   . . . .
   a. discount   **b.** price   **c.** account   **d.** amount

5. The deal fell . . . . because they were offered a better price by our competitors.
   a. off   **b.** through   **c.** over   **d.** across

6. We built . . . . our chain of stores, starting with one small store.
   a. on   **b.** out   **c.** across   **d.** up

7. You are in danger of being . . . . for negligence if you don't improve your safety standards.
   a. sued   **b.** courted   **c.** sown   **d.** caught

8. New cars are usually . . . . onto the market in a blaze of publicity.
   a. fired   **b.** set   **c.** launched   **d.** sent

9. The countryside is being polluted by industrial . . . .
   a. waste   **b.** waist   **c.** garbage   **d.** wastage

10. If you need a loan, your bank is sure to ask you for some kind of . . . .
    a. proof   **b.** property   **c.** collateral   **d.** assurance

11. If you require any further details, please do not . . . . to contact us.
    a. hesitate   **b.** doubt   **c.** stop   **d.** think

12. Pay your staff well and worker . . . . will increase.
    a. production   **b.** products   **c.** productivity   **d.** producing

13. Bad . . . . flow is bad news for any company!
    a. money   **b.** monetary   **c.** finance   **d.** cash

14. Thank goodness somebody invented the solar- . . . . calculator!
    a. electric   **b.** energy   **c.** powered   **d.** electronic

15. Our policy is keep prices low and stay . . . .
    a. competitive   **b.** competing   **c.** repetitive   **d.** winning

Test 2 – Units 15 – 28

Choose the best alternative to complete each example:

1. Efficiency has shown a . . . . improvement over the past six months.
   a. signified   **b.** marked   **c.** distinguished   **d.** repeated

2. The job is only temporary until I find something more . . . .
   a. final   **b.** basic   **c.** permanent   **d.** solid

3. A healthy national economy depends on the government's attitude towards private . . . .
   a. enterprise   **b.** business   **c.** concerns   **d.** initiatives

4. We offer a wide . . . . of different products to meet different needs.
   a. group   **b.** selection   **c.** lot   **d.** amount

5. I'd like to reserve a room . . . . the name of Christensen.
   a. on   **b.** in   **c.** at   **d.** under

6. We apologize for the . . . . this mistake caused you.
   a. inconvenience   **b.** disturbance   **c.** upset   **d.** perplexity

7. Before ordering anything, first get three different . . . .
   a. bids   **b.** biddings   **c.** quotations   **d.** attempts

8. The higher the risk, the more your insurance . . . . costs you.
   a. price   **b.** premium   **c.** cost   **d.** tariff

9. This year's results were excellent. They more than . . . . up for last year's losses.
   a. took   **b.** did   **c.** put   **d.** made

10. We've been . . . . really good business in the Philippines since we opened our office in Manila.
    a. doing   **b.** making   **c.** having   **d.** effecting

11. You must be pleased with yourself. You've . . . . your business a great success.
    a. done   **b.** taken   **c.** made   **d.** had

12. It's terrible! I just can't figure it out. Our talks with the unions seem to be going . . . .
    a. anywhere   **b.** somewhere   **c.** nowhere   **d.** whereabouts

13. We regret the . . . . in processing your order, but we promise you will receive it very soon.
    a. delay   **b.** pause   **c.** stay   **d.** lag

14. Thank goodness business seems to be . . . .
    a. getting up   **b.** picking off   **c.** setting off   **d.** picking up

15. I'm sorry to have to ask you to send my order . . . . such short notice.
    a. on   **b.** at   **c.** with   **d.** in

Test 3 – Units 29 – 42

Choose the best alternative to complete each example:

1. Entrance to our R&D department is . . . . limited to staff members only.
   a. strictly   **b.** formally   **c.** closely   **d.** privately

2. It's the job of the PR Department to make sure we project the right . . . .
   a. picture   **b.** sense   **c.** image   **d.** appearance

3. Our standard payment . . . . are strictly 30 days from invoice date.
   a. rules   **b.** terms   **c.** regulations   **d.** concessions

4. Our staff is well-qualified, well-paid, and . . . .
   a. highly practiced   **b.** well-trained   **c.** highly trained   **d.** well-exercised

5. After falling throughout the morning stock prices . . . . ground steadily by the close of trading.
   a. gained   **b.** won   **c.** found   **d.** improved

6. We provide an . . . . leaflet with all our products, giving a list of service centers world-wide.
   a. explaining   **b.** detailing   **c.** explanatory   **d.** illustrating

7. In our high-tech world, companies must be on their guard against industrial . . . .
   a. spying   **b.** espionage   **c.** detection   **d.** disclosures

8. Ordinary shareholders are . . . . to vote at the meeting.
   a. approved   **b.** warranted   **c.** authorized   **d.** entitled

9. Every company wishes it had several . . . . cows to see it through the bad times.
   a. money   **b.** milk   **c.** financial   **d.** cash

10. We insist on giving people a . . . . training before letting them loose on Joe Public.
    a. through   **b.** thorough   **c.** absolute   **d.** whole

11. Could you please send me . . . . details and an application form.
    a. further   **b.** farther   **c.** more   **d.** extra

12. I . . . . a check for $20 and the completed form.
    a. include   **b.** contain   **c.** enclose   **d.** endorse

13. We're going through a difficult time. All employees will have to . . . . unnecessary expenditures.
    a. stop in on   **b.** cut down on   **c.** take down on   **d.** put down on

14. The last thing our accounts department wants is to be . . . . by the government.
    a. accounted   **b.** audited   **c.** inquired into   **d.** surveyed

15. IBM is one of the biggest . . . . companies in the world today.
    a. multi-country   **b.** pan-global   **c.** multi-national   **d.** inter-country

Test 4 – Units 43 – 56

Choose the best alternative to complete each example:

1. We hope the days of . . . . strikes are over!
   a. wild dog   **b.** madcap   **c.** wildcat   **d.** black rat

2. I was full of admiration . . . . the way the inquiry was handled.
   a. on   **b.** for   **c.** in   **d.** at

3. By the way, congratulations . . . . winning the airport contract!
   a. on   **b.** for   **c.** at   **d.** in

4. The . . . . study shows that the bay is the ideal place to start building.
   a. possibility   **b.** potentiality   **c.** viability   **d.** feasibility

5. Our R&D Manager is in . . . . of a young and highly talented team.
   a. lead   **b.** head   **c.** charge   **d.** top

6. Always read an insurance . . . . before you sign it!
   a. contract   **b.** document   **c.** policy   **d.** polity

7. I think we'd better . . . . steps to make sure this does not happen again!
   a. make   **b.** take   **c.** do   **d.** produce

8. Just wait and see how the new miniature version starts selling like . . . .
   a. hot buns   **b.** hot potatoes   **c.** hot dogs   **d.** hotcakes

9. I would like to consult my colleague – that way I'm leaving my . . . . open.
   a. chances   **b.** possibilities   **c.** options   **d.** opportunities

10. I don't believe anyone gets job . . . . from working on an assembly line, do you?
    a. satisfaction   **b.** comfort   **c.** relief   **d.** happiness

11. In faraway markets it's often best to think of . . . . your product to avoid high shipping costs.
    a. leasing   **b.** covenanting   **c.** licensing   **d.** contracting

12. Nobody is really responsible for making decisions on advertising. I wish it wasn't such a . . . . area.
    a. brown   **b.** green   **c.** gray   **d.** murky

13. Accounts which are settled promptly are eligible . . . . a 5% discount.
    a. to   **b.** for   **c.** with   **d.** into

14. We need someone who is capable . . . . using Spanish and Portuese on a daily basis.
    a. to   **b.** of   **c.** with   **d.** in

15. Our latest marketing campaign is really setting the . . . . in our field.
    a. pace   **b.** speed   **c.** trap   **d.** running

Test 5 – Units 57 – 68

Choose the best alternative to complete each example:

1. How well do you get . . . . with the other people in your section?
   a. in　　　　**b.** along　　　　**c.** on　　　　　　**d.** up

2. We are trialling some new tests to measure the . . . . of applicants for vacancies.
   a. attitude　　**b.** success　　**c.** aptitude　　　**d.** talent

3. We use a standardized form to make sure we get all the . . . . we need before we interview candidates.
   a. particulars　**b.** peculiarities　**c.** specialities　　**d.** informations

4. I am not in a . . . . to comment on why you are losing your job.
   a. place　　　**b.** space　　　**c.** situation　　　**d.** position

5. The payments were made through your bank in . . . . with our signed contract.
   a. agreement　**b.** accord　　　**c.** accordance　　**d.** consent

6. 'It's the real thing.' – one of the best advertising . . . . of all time!
   a. sentences　**b.** lyrics　　　**c.** slogans　　　**d.** phrases

7. Please accept the enclosed . . . . tickets to our 'Meet the Celebrity' breakfast on the closing morning of the convention.
   a. compliment　**b.** gratuitous　**c.** complimentary　**d.** grateful

8. It's not a hard and fast rule, but as a rule of . . . . I'd always advise making appointments in advance.
   a. finger　　　**b.** fist　　　　**c.** toe　　　　　**d.** thumb

9. All wording on cigarette packs have to . . . . with the new regulations.
   a. imply　　　**b.** comply　　　**c.** reply　　　　**d.** supply

10. If we do not receive the goods by tomorrow, you will be in . . . . of our agreement.
    a. breach　　**b.** fault　　　　**c.** failure　　　**d.** violation

11. If a task is routine, do your best to . . . . it to someone else.
    a. trust　　　**b.** transfer　　**c.** delegate　　　**d.** refuse

12. One of the chief roles of management is to keep staff . . . .
    a. exercised　**b.** motivated　**c.** generated　　**d.** energized

13. The . . . . in this department has sunk to an all time low. Let's do something about it!
    a. morality　**b.** mortality　　**c.** morale　　　**d.** moral

14. I can't give you an exact estimate, but I should imagine something in the area of $50,000 would be a . . . . figure.
    a. precise　　**b.** imprecise　　**c.** state of the art　**d.** ballpark

15. Our turnover is running . . . . with Alamo at the moment.
    a. toe and toe　**b.** hand and hand　**c.** neck and neck　**d.** head and head

Answers

1. 1.high-rise 2.answer the phone, attend a conference, cash a check, join a team, program a computer 3.competitors, competition, competitive, competitively 4.drew, led, rose, spread 5.approximately, Company, Automated Teller Machine, Free On Board (sometimes written f.o.b.), Post Office Box, North American Free Trade Agreement 6.gone, gear, food, height

2. 1.campaign, classified ad., commercial slogan 2.check in, reservation, room service, weekend rate 3.apply for, interview, overtime, training, 4.agenda, CEO, chairperson, minutes 5.exchange rate, owe, profit, refund 6.fax, filing cabinet, stapler, computer

3. 1.calendar 2.filing cabinet 3.umbrella 4.monitor 5.printer 6.files 7.phone 8.keyboard 9.appointment book 10. passport 11.vase 12.eraser 13.pen 14.pencil 15.map 16.check book

4. 1.Dear 2.advertisement 3.current issue 4.latest catalog 5.price list 6.forward 7.Sincerely 8.regards 9.information 10.particularly 11.model 12.still available 13.advise 14.payment 15.discount 16.price range

5. Set 1 1.e 2.d 3.c 4.a 5.g 6.f 7.b 8.h Set 2 1.h 2.a 3.d 4.e 5.f 6.b 7.g 8.c 1.offer a discount 2.make a profit 3.raise capital 4.call a meeting

6. 1.cut ... off 2.found out 3.kept ... down 4.came out 5.read ... back 6.fell through 7.though ... over 8.got through 9.built ... up 10.broke down 11.sold out 12.shut down 13.went on 14.drove up 15.took off 16.heard from

7. 1.c 2.d 3.j 4.i 5.b 6.k 7.l 8.h 9.a 10.f 11.g 12.e 1.industrial espionage 2.book a flight 3.settled their accounts 4.launch a new product 5.out to dinner

8. 1.advertising 2.affect 3.lend 4.postpone 5.inspected 6.delayed 7.economics 8.interested 9.job 10.waste 11.living 12.measurements 13.rise 14.receipt 15.remind 16.tell 17.sensitive 18.stationery

9. 1.withdraw 2.ATM 3.issued 4.debited 5.credit rating 6.financial institutions 7.commission 8.statement 9.in full 10.interest 11.outstanding 12.loan 13.collateral 14.default 15.overdraft 16.bounce

10. 1.e 2.i 3.a 4.j 5.l 6.b 7.k 8.c 9.h 10.d 11.g 12.f

11. 1.inquiry 2.pleasure 3.further details 4.hesitate 5.Sincerely 6.full details 7.supply 8.inquiring 9.in production 10.enclosed leaflet 11.additional features 12.competitive price 13.selection 14.In addition 15.date 16.doing business

12. 1.h 2.f 3.m 4.d 5.k 6.c 7.n 8.i 9.l 10.b 11.a 12.g 13.e 14.o 15.j 1.word processor 2.office building 3.exchange rate 4.customer satisfaction

13. 1.laser printer 2.answering machine 3.burglar alarm 4.cordless phone 5.fax machine 6.computer 7.daily planner 8.office chair 9.pager 10.photocopier 11.signmaking kit 12.clock 13.briefcase 14.pocket calculator 15.pen 16.table lamp

14. 1.unacceptable, acceptance 2.action, active, activity 3.additions, additional 4.analysis, analysts 5.applicant, application, applicable 6.assistance, assistant 7. attractions, attractive 8.commercial, commercially, commercialized, commercials 9.connecting, connection, connections 10.contractor, contractually 11.directions, directors, directory, directly, directive 12.indecisive, decision 13.competitors, competition, competitive 14.distributor, distribution 15.economize, economists

15. 1.partial 2.approximate 3.internal 4.low 5.light 6.short 7.mandatory 8.full-time 9.negative 10.private 11.complex 12.marked 13.basic 14.permanent

16. Set 1 1.a 2.h 3.b 4.e 5.g 6.f 7.f 8.c Set 2 1.a 2.b 3.e 4.d 5.h 6.c 7.f 8.g 1.introductory offer 2.annual conference 3.early retirement 4.skilled workers

17. 1.c 2.e 3.g 4.j 5.d 6.k 7.n 8.b 9.l 10.m 11.i 12.h 13.a 14.f

18. 1.current issue 2.shipping 3.quotation 4.selection 5.terms 6.following 7.note 8.reserve the right 9.accept delivery 10.acknowledge 11.line 12.regret 13.resume 14.inconvenience 15.supply 16.inventory

19. 1.compatible, data, E-mail, software 2.lay-offs, mediate, picket, strike 3.adjuster, claim, policyholder, premium 4.dumping, embargo, export, tariff 5.portfolio, shares, speculate, stock exchange 6.judge, legal, sue, trial

20. 1.accurate 2.retrieve 3.supplies 4.components 5.transactions 6.records 7.peripherals 8.graphics 9.memory 10.drive 11.back-up 12.publishing 13.display 14.printer 15.networking 16.on-line

21. 1.make 2.do 3.make 4.made 5.do 6.doing 7.made 8.make 9.doing 10.made 11.do 12.make 13.make 14.make 15.do 16.done 17.made 18.done

22. 1.j 2.b 3.k 4.a 5.h 6.i 7.c 8.g 9.e 10.f 11.l 12.d

23. 1.set 2.issue 3.guaranteed delivery 4.passed 5.deducted 6.matter 7.further delay 8.response 9.refund 10.obliged 11.regret the delay 12.processing 13.dealing 14.misplaced 15.apologize for 16.deter

24. 1.b 2.b 3.b 4.c 5.d 6.a 7.b 8.a 9.c 10.c 11.a 12.c 13.b 14.c 15.c 16.b

25. 1.give 2.spend 3.budget 4.save 5.invest 6.waste 7.buy 8.borrow 9.make 10.find 11.lost 12.spare

26. 1.Directors 2.Officer 3.President 4.Finance 5.Corporate 6.Advertising 7.Resources 8.Data 9.Development 10.Strategic 11.Research 12.Division

27. A 1.pointer 2.overhead projector 3.slide projector 4.handout 5.felt tip pen 6.screen 7.pie chart 8.line graph 9.bar graph 10.podium 11.notes 12.microphone 13.curtain 14.flip chart

27. B 1.Let me start 2.on such short notice 3.As you know 4.purpose 5.up to date 6.First of all 7.Next 8.Finally 9.priorities 10.Draw your attention 11. As far as 12.as a whole 13.On the contrary 14.On the other hand 15.In other words 16.to sum up

28. Set 1 1.e 2.b 3.g 4.c 5.h 6.d 7.f 8.a Set 2 1.e 2.b 3.f 4.h 5.g 6.a 7.c 8.d 1.reduce costs 2.Launch a product 3.settle disputes 4.build a factory

29. 1.conveniently 2.satisfactorily 3.widely 4.fully 5.financially 6.specially 7.eventually 8.absolutely 9.strictly 10.considerably 11.correctly 12.temporarily 13.virtually 14.tactfully 15.favorably 16.environmentally

30. 1.b 2.c 3.a 4.d 5.a 6.c 7.a 8.b 9.a 10.b 11.c 12.a 13.d 14.c 15.c

31. 1.complimentary copy 2.recent publications 3.highly popular 4.extensively tested 5.favorable response 6.suitable 7.recommend 8.experience 9.needs 10.featured 11.payment terms 12.further information 13.representatives 14.specially selected 15.value 16.confident 17.colleagues 18.subscription form 19.convenience 20.eligible

32. Set 1 1.g 2.e 3.b 4.f 5.c 6.a 7.d 8.h Set 2 1.b 2.a 3.e 4.g 5.h 6.d 7.f 8.c 1.mouth-watering recipes 2.highly-trained staff 3.perfect fit 4.stress-free driving

33. 1.rejected 2.demolishing 3.attacked 4.withdraw 5.accept 6.succeed 7.imposed 8.gained 9.lost 10.keep 11.lower 12.increase 13.complicate 14.strengthen 15.expanded 16.agreed

34. 1.unemployment, employee, employer, employment 2.expensive, expenses, expenditure, expense 3.explanatory, explanation 4.extended, extension, extensively, extent 5.financial, financially 6.growing, growth 7.impression, impressive, unimpressed 8.industrial, industrialist, industrialized 9.inflated, inflation, inflationary 10.information, informative, misinformed 11.instructions, instruction 12.introductory, introduction 13.investment, investors 14.knowledge, unknown, knowledgeable 15.illegal, legality

35. 1.purchase (buy) 2.perceive (see) 3.elapsed (passed) 4.facilitate (ease) 5.require (need) 6.terminate (end) 7.anticipate (expect) 8.possess (have) 9.comprehend (understand)

36. 1.b 2.d 3.a 4.b 5.b 6.a 7.d 8.a 9.c 10.d 11.c 12.d 13.a 14.a

37. 1.d 2.g 3.k 4.j 5.l 6.a 7.i 8.b 9.e 10.h 11.c 12.f

38. A 1.kitchen staff 2.outgoing 3.hard work 4.suit 5.contact 6.required 7.busy office 8.preference 9.willing 10.initiative 11.clear 12.thorough training 13.potential customers 14.successful candidate 15.experience 16.skills 17.ability 18.team 19.competitive 20.pension plan B 1.to 2.in 3.position 4.further 5.form 6.for 7.enclose 8.as 9.audio 10.with 11.inquiries 12.take 13.opportunity 14.available 15.consider 16.favorably

39. 1.ran out 2.carried out 3.set up 4.stood in 5.cut down 6.stopped over/off 7.drew up 8.wrote off 9.relied on 10.gave in 11.left out 12.laid off 13.stuck to 14.paid back

40. 1.a 2.b 3.b 4.c 5.b 6.a 7.b 8.b 9.b 10.d 11.a 12.d 13.b 14.a 15.c

41. 1.confident 2.relevant 3.efficient 4.insolvent 5.permanent 6.significant 7.excellent 8.convenient 9.constant 10.current 11.dominant 12.consistent 13.extravagant 14.reluctant 15.dependent

42. Set 1 1.h 2.f 3.b 4.d 5.e 6.g 7.c 8.a Set 2 1.h 2.a 3.b 4.f 5.c 6.g 7.d 8.e 1.alternative arrangements 2.multi-national company 3.potential customer 4.close attention

43. 1.a 2.c 3.d 4.a 5.c 6.b 7.a 8.c 9.c 10.a 11.c 12.b 13.c 14.c 15.d

44. 1.date stamp 2.guillotine 3.note pad 4.paper clips 5.pencil sharpener 6.hole punch 7.ruler 8.scale 9.scissors 10.stamps 11.stapler 12.staples 13.adding machine 14.tray 15.waste basket 16.calculator

45. 1.admiration for 2.effect on 3.access to 4.confidence in 5.solution to 6.interest in 7.chance of 8.emphasis on 9.experience of 10.point in 11.increase in 12.intention of 13.congratulations on 14.result of

46. 1.g 2.i 3.n 4.c 5.k 6.p 7.j 8.o 9.d 10.l 11.e 12.b 13.f 14.m 15.h 16.a 1.productivity bonus 2.assembly line 3.takeover bid 4.market research 5.salary scale 6.balance sheet

47. 1.R&D Manager 2.personnel officer 3.draughtsperson 4.clerk 5.assembly person 6.sales representative 7.accountant 8.chauffeur 9.auto mechanic 10.receptionist 11.computer operator 12.advertising executive 1.existing selection 2.essential member 3.nightshift 4.pragmatic approach 5.clean driver's license 6.main responsibilities

48. 1.b 2.b 3.c 4.b 5.b 6.b 7.a 8.c 9.b 10.d 11.d 12.a 13.a 14.b

49. 1.take out 2.take on 3.taken ... consideration 4.took off 5.take home 6.take ... call 7.take steps 8.take ... chair 9.take ... seriously 10.take ... down 11.taken over 12.take ... further 13.take charge 14.taking ... risk 15.took notes

50. 1.selling like hotcakes 2.word-of-mouth 3.went belly-up 4.head-to-head 5.a niche 6.number-crunching 7.market globalization 8.breaking even 9.going public 10.on the cutting edge 11.politically correct 12.took a nose dive 13. fall by the wayside 14.through the grapevine

51. 1.advice 2.briefly 3.seat 4.check 5.complimentary 6.conform 7.confidential 8.conscientious 9.economic 10.refund 11.fee 12.income 13.research 14.competition 15.notes 16.takeover 17.price 18.productivity

52. 1.management, Manager, manageable 2.negotiable, negotiations 3.unoccupied, occupational 4.operation, operating, operational, operator 5.optional, options 6.originally, originated, originality 7.preference, preferred 8.production, product, unproductive, productivity 9.unprofitable, profitability 10.restrictions, restrictive, restricted 11.satisfaction, satisfactory, dissatisfied 12.systematic, systematically 13.suitability, suitable 14.variety, variable, various

53. 1.b 2.c 3.d 4.c 5.c 6.a 7.c 8.a 9.b 10.c 11.b 12.a 13.b 14.a 15.d

54. 1.black 2.black 3.green 4.blue 5.black ... white 6.gray 7.red 9.gray 10.red 11.blue 12.white 13.blue 14.red 15.white 16.black

55. 1.familiar with 2.eligible for 3.available for 4.envious of 5.Contrary to 6.popular with 7.consistent with 8.responsible for 9.aware of 10.capable of 11.relevant to 12.accustomed to 13.acceptable to 14.dependent on 15.proud of 16.well-known for

56. Set 1 1.b 2.f 3.g 4.e 5.a 6.c 7.h 8.d Set 2 1.h 2.f 3.a 4.e 5.b 6.c 7.g 8.d 1.set the pace 2.pay duty 3.consult a lawyer 4.transfer funds

57. 1.b 2.b 3.d 4.b 5.b 6.d 7.a 8.d 9.c 10.a 11.c 12.b 13.c 14.d 15.a 16.c 17.c 18.a 19.c 20.b 21.d 22.b 23.d 24.b 25.b 26.a 27.c 28.a

58. 1.in a position to 2.in accordance with 3.in circulation 4.in debt 5.in charge of 6.in advance 7.in stock 8.in error 9.in due course 10.in the process of 11.in mind 12.in transit

59. 1.b 2.d 3.a 4.b 5.d 6.a 7.b 8.a 9.d 10.a 11.c 12.b 13.d 14.a

60. 1.pleased 2.complimentary tickets 3.up to date 4.ideal opportunity 5.comprehensive selection 6.new feature 7.series of lectures 8.speakers 9.emphasis 10.field 11.in-depth discussion 12.enclosed map 13.conveniently situated 14.enter 15.company details 16.look forward

61. 1.contract 2.practice 3.thumb 4.absence 5.earnings 6.error 7.mouth 8.embarkation 9.return 10.charges 11.hands 12.living 1.rate of return 2.rule of thumb 3.breach of contract 4.show of hands 5.code of practice

62. 1.h 2.i 3.e 4.j 5.k 6.b 7.a 8.c 9.f 10.g 11.l 12.d

63. 1.b 2.c 3.a 4.d 5.c 6.d 7.b 8.a 9.a 10.c 11.b 12.a 13.d 14.a 15.d

64. 1.systematically 2.readily 3.financially 4.consistently 5.formally 6.absolutely 7.firmly 8.convincingly 9.irretrievably 10.initially 11.adversely 12.instataneously 13. highly 14.unpredictably

65. 1.training sessions 2.suitable 3.requirements 4.single 5.provide 6.quotation 7.full board 8.brochure 9.meet 10.reasonable rates 11.available 12.urge 13.without delay 14.require 15.hesitate 16.pleasure

66. 1.unnecessary paperwork 2.separate folders 3.members of staff 4.Set priorities 5.put off unpleasant tasks 6.lose concentration 7.Delegate routine tasks 8.time-consuming way 9.have a meeting 10.set a time limit 11.Skip over 12.pick out

67. 1.b 2.c 3.d 4.c 5.a 6.b 7.c 8.b 9.c 10.a 11.d 12.b 13.c 14.b 15.a

68. 1.rebound 2.rain check 3.sales pitch 4.ballpark figure 5.play hardball 6.heavyweights 7.major player 8.struck out 9.right off the bat 10.in the running 11.touch base 12.by the rules 13.neck and neck 14.inside track 15.team work

Test 1	1.b 2.c 3.c 4.a 5.b 6.d 7.a 8.c 9.a 10.c 11.a 12.c 13.d 14.c 15.a
Test 2	1.b 2.c 3.a 4.b 5.d 6.a 7.c 8.b 9.d 10.a 11.c 12.c 13.a 14.d 15.a
Test 3	1.a 2.c 3.b 4.c 5.a 6.c 7.b 8.d 9.d 10.b 11.a or c 12.c 13.b 14.b 15.c
Test 4	1.c 2.b 3.a 4.d 5.c 6.c 7.b 8.d 9.c 10.a 11.c 12.c 13.b 14.b 15.d
Test 5	1.b 2.c 3.a 4.d 5.c 6.c 7.c 8.d 9.b 10.a 11.c 12.b 13.c 14.d 15.c